Healthy Snacks for Kids

Penny Warner

BRISTOL PUBLISHING ENTERPRISES
Hayward, California

A nitty gritty® cookbook

Printed in the United States of America.

ISBN 13: 978-1-55867-336-6

ISBN 10: 1-55867-336-9

Cover design: Frank J. Paredes
Cover photography: John A. Benson
Food stylist: Randy Mon
Illustrations: James Balkovek

CONTENTS

1	Smuggle Good Things Into Every Meal
2	Ten Ways to Make Your Child a Healthy Eater
6	The New Food Pyramid
9	Healthful Hints
11	Have Fun With Feeding
14	Super Snacks
46	Dynamite Drinks
70	Frozen Fun
95	Better Breakfasts
117	Marvelous Meals

SMUGGLE GOOD THINGS INTO EVERY MEAL

"Snack time!" The words are magic to a child's ear. But to a parent, they can present a real challenge. You may reach a point when you don't know what to do to get your child to eat nutritious foods. Try as you might to introduce high fiber foods and leafy greens, your child refuses to have any part of them.

There is plenty of evidence that nutrition is important for good health now and later in life. Studies even indicate that eating the right foods prevents some diseases. You will give your child the gift of better health if you encourage healthy eating habits that he or she can carry into the future.

When all else fails, try trickery! Be sneaky with the picky eater and pump up breakfasts, snacks and meals with nutritious ingredients. Your child will develop a taste for healthy foods and you will gradually influence and encourage healthy eating.

With the help of the many ideas and recipes in this collection, you can establish a lifetime of good eating habits for your child. To make your job easier, the recipes in this book are high in nutrition, easy to prepare, inexpensive, low in or free of sugar and salt and loved by kids.

TEN WAYS TO MAKE YOUR CHILD A HEALTHY EATER

1. SMUGGLE NUTRITIOUS FOODS INTO OLD FAVORITES.

Mix chopped spinach into turkey burgers, grated carrots into peanut butter and cooked zucchini into pancakes. Add a little wheat germ to pizza dough, cookies and even smoothies. Be creative with your trickery — you'll surprise yourself.

2. GIVE FOOD SILLY NAMES.

Children love whimsical things and will usually try something new if it has a funny name. What kid could resist a glass of "Mooseberry Juice" or a "Banana Wiggle"?

3. LET KIDS HELP.

Even small children can help in the preparation of some of the things they eat. Children who help make their snacks are more likely to eat them. Better yet, teach children how to grow their own vegetables in the backyard garden.

4. EDUCATE YOUR CHILD ABOUT THE FOOD PYRAMID.

Talk about foods that help children grow strong and stay healthy — and those that don't. Classify foods at the market or on the table into the food groups of the food pyramid. Play simple games that teach about these foods.

5. THINK SMALL.

It's not so overwhelming to a child when there are small amounts on a plate, or small bites to eat. A child will ask for more if desired. Sometimes it's fun to make a face or a design with the food. Try anything to create a happy atmosphere and stimulate a child's imagination.

6. GO EASY ON SUGAR AND SALT.

Try to omit sugar and salt from the recipes you make, or at least decrease the amount used. The results may not taste as good to you, but if your child is raised with limited amounts of sugar and salt, she or he will never miss them. Use alternatives, such as dates and raisins, whenever possible. If you feel you must use a sweetener, use honey instead of sugar — it's sweeter so you don't need to use as much. Keep salt and sugar off the table, and look for unsweetened products at the market.

7. LET PROPS HELP SELL WHAT YOU'RE SERVING.

Kids love bright colors, animals, clowns, funny straws and above all, variety. A different plate or a funny bowl with a picture on it just might stimulate a child's desire to try something new. Avoid the same old thing. Collect a variety of small colorful plates, cups, bowls, glasses and place mats.

8. MAKE MEALTIME AND SNACK TIME A PLEASANT SOCIAL EVENT.

A child is much more apt to try new things under these circumstances. Don't get angry — it only makes a child more stubborn. Maybe he or she simply isn't hungry, but will be a willing eater at the next meal. Try to avoid pleading ("Please eat"), threatening ("No dessert if you don't eat your salad") or guilt-inducing ("Think of all the hungry children in the world"). These tactics won't help in the long run. Ask your child to try everything. Don't force him or her to finish everything.

9. DON'T NEGLECT DAIRY PRODUCTS.

Substitute low-fat or nonfat dairy products for those made with whole milk. Use reduced fat or nonfat cheeses, especially when there are several other ingredients in a recipe. Experiment with nonfat cheeses to find those that melt well. Some regular cheeses are naturally lower in fat, such as part-skim mozzarella and Parmesan.

10. CUT BACK ON FATS.

Turkey lunch meats are good low-fat substitutes for bologna, salami and other lunch meats. When a recipe calls for nuts or seeds, you may want to reduce the quantity (they have lots of fiber, but unfortunately are high in fat). You'll find that cutting back on the fats in a recipe frequently doesn't affect the overall flavor!

ABOUT FATS

- Fats add flavor and transport vitamins to body tissues, but you only need a little.
- Cut down on butter, mayonnaise, salad dressing, meat, fried food, gravies, whole milk, cheese, and nuts.
- Use nonstick spray when frying or buttering a dish; Sauté in broth or nonstick spray, or use polyunsaturated oil such as corn, safflower, or sunflower.
- Reduce high-fat dairy products to low-fat: such as, whole milk to lowfat or nonfat milk; heavy cream to half-and-half
- Instead of butter, try one of the new, non-hydrogenated, no-trans-fat butter substitutes like 'Smart Balance'. These are a big improvement over margarine.
- Broil, bake, steam or barbecue your meat – avoid frying.

THE NEW FOOD PYRAMID

The new food pyramid, instead of being divided top-to-bottom, with grains on the bottom, is cut into vertical slices, to emphasize the importance of all the food groups. The 'three dimensional' element — the staircase on the left side — is to integrate the importance of exercise to health and diet.

The new food pyramid also attempts to modify the impression (by its appearing at the base of the pyramid) that we can eat unregulated amounts of pasta and rice.

THE BASICS OF HEALTHY EATING

This is a list of good basic foods children should be encouraged to eat. If a child learns to enjoy them early, he or she will be a healthy eater for life.

Use these foods interchangeably in the recipes in this book, and use the recipes as a guideline for your own ideas. For example, instead of sneaking spinach into turkey burgers (*Popeye Burgers,* page 148), hide pureed peas or green beans in meat loaf mix.

BREAD, CEREAL, RICE AND PASTA GROUP

- air-popped popcorn
- bagels
- bran cereals
- brown rice
- cornbread
- crackers
- English muffins
- low-fat granola
- macaroni
- oatmeal
- spaghetti
- whole grain breads

VEGETABLE GROUP

- broccoli
- carrots
- cauliflower
- celery
- corn
- fresh beans
- green bell peppers
- peas
- potatoes
- red bell peppers
- spinach
- squash
- sweet potatoes
- tomatoes
- zucchini

FRUIT GROUP

- apricots
- avocadoes
- berries
- cherries
- citrus fruits
- dried fruits
- kiwis
- mangoes
- melons
- papayas
- peaches
- pears
- pineapples
- plums
- prunes

MILK, CHEESE AND YOGURT GROUP

- buttermilk
- low-fat cottage cheese
- low-fat fruit-flavored yogurt
- low-fat ice cream
- low-fat or nonfat milk
- low-fat ricotta cheese
- Parmesan cheese
- part-skim mozzarella cheese
- yogurt cheese

MEAT, POULTRY, FISH, DRY BEANS, EGGS AND NUTS GROUP

- chicken
- extra-lean ham
- peanuts or reduced fat peanut butter
- lean beef
- lentils
- split peas

- beans: pinto, kidney, garbanzo, etc.
- shrimp
- tofu
- water-packed tuna
- turkey
- walnuts

HEALTHFUL HINTS

- Children must eat often due to their bodies' demand for high energy. Serve them 3 meals and 2 to 3 healthy snacks each day on a regular schedule. Don't overdo it, however. Children should learn to experience hunger instead of constantly feeling full.
- Carob is a good substitute for chocolate because it doesn't contain caffeine.
- Whole wheat flour can be substituted for white flour in most recipes. If you don't want to use all whole wheat, replace part of the white flour with whole wheat

flour. You will be adding important fiber to your family's diet. Use whole grain bread whenever possible.

- Use yogurt cheese instead of cream cheese: Drain 1 qt. nonfat, gelatin-free plain yogurt in a yogurt cheese maker or through a paper coffee filter suspended in a tall container. Refrigerate for 24 hours or until thick. Discard the liquid (whey). Makes about 2 cups.
- Emphasize citrus fruits in your child's diet. They are rich in vitamin C and provide important nutrients for growing bodies. Try one of the calcium-fortified orange juices on the market for strengthening little bones. Whenever possible, opt for whole fruits instead of fruit juices to add fiber.
- Look for fruits and vegetables that are brilliantly colored. A good rule of thumb is that the brighter in color the fruit or vegetable, the more nutrients it contains. For example, choose romaine lettuce instead of iceberg because its green color is much deeper.
- Use only one high fat ingredient in each dish. Nonfat items are good choices for mixing with several other ingredients in a recipe. The other flavors in the dish compensate for blandness.

- Use refrigerated pizza dough instead of biscuit dough when making pigs-in-a-blanket or other children's favorites. Biscuit dough gets about 50% of its calories from fat, while pizza dough derives only 14% of its calories from fat.
- Dairy products are important for a young person's growth. If you select milk products that are low-fat or nonfat, your child will get all of the benefits of dairy without unneeded fat and cholesterol. Hard cheeses are generally more flavorful, so you don't need to use as much.
- The most important thing you can do to make your child a healthy eater is to set a good example. Kids watch their parents for clues on how to behave. If you don't eat well, it's unreasonable to expect them to do so.

HAVE FUN WITH FEEDING

- Try new things early. You'd be amazed: many two- and three-year-olds really enjoy avocadoes, seaweed, hummus (experiment: some brands may be too garlicky for little kids) and pita bread, soybeans (known as edamame), rice milk, soy milk, and other healthy, nutritious snack foods. You may even find that they are more open-minded than you are, and will cause you to try new foods. And if you start them early, it's much easier to keep going on the right path.

- Make toast faces: spread toast with yogurt cheese or peanut butter, and use nuts, raisins, coconut, dried fruit bits or pieces of vegetables to make faces.
- If your child carries a lunch box, tuck in a surprise: a new pencil, a cheerful note, a fancy straw — use your imagination.
- Use cookie cutters to cut out bread for fanciful sandwiches.
- Splurge on some bright paper products; colorful cartons, straws and napkins dress up a meal or a snack.
- Add pleasant music to mealtime or snack time. Discourage television viewing while children are eating.
- Stuff sandwich fillings into different edible holders. Bell peppers, cored apples, ice cream cones, waffle squares, cooked giant pasta shells, pancakes, hollowed tomatoes and hollowed dinner rolls are all fun choices.
- Make cottage cheese or yogurt "sundaes" in cantaloupe or honeydew melon halves. Top with granola and a cherry.
- Make "boats" out of raw snow pea pods and fill with sandwich fillings. Make "sails" out of green bell pepper pieces.

NUTRITIONAL ANALYSIS

This book offers a brief nutritional analysis for each recipe*. The analysis is presented for the smallest number of servings indicated in each recipe unless otherwise specified. Optional ingredients are not calculated in the analysis. If a choice of ingredients is offered, the first ingredient is analyzed. For recipes using yogurt cheese, refer to the recipe under '**Healthful Hints'**, on page 10.

A graphic representation of the new food pyramid is shown for each recipe, indicating the food group(s) that are emphasized. This does not mean that that group's servings are adequate for the day, but only that the group is represented in this recipe. *Recipes were analyzed using The Food Processor, available from ESHA Research, www.esha.com.

FAT INTAKE

Opinions differ on the amount of fat calories youngsters should eat. Some authorities recommend that they keep their fat intake between 30% and 40% of their daily calories. Other experts, however, recommend that children, like adults, should consume no more than 30% of their daily calories in the form of fat. Most agree that parents should not restrict fat intake for children under 2 years.

SUPER SNACKS

15 Apple Snow

16 Yummy Yogurt

17 Cheesy Popovers

18 Munchkins

19 Hot Nibbles

20 Silly Salad

21 Fruity Popcorn

22 Date Cookies

23 Peanut Butter Muffins

24 Jack's Beanstalks

25 Spumoni Celery

26 Banana Oatsies

27 Fruit Cobbler Crunch

28 Pita Parfait

29 Oven Apples

30 Super Hero Snacks

31 Apple Smacks

32 Yogurt Plus

34 Hot Cheese Funnies

35 Fruit Chewies

36 Hawaiian Rollers

37 Banana Bombs

38 Flying Saucers

39 Monkey Bars

40 Applenutties

41 Baked Veggie Spread

42 Zippety Dips

43 Chili Dip

45 Cottage Cheese Dip

45 Fruit Dip

APPLE SNOW

A light and fluffy snack or dessert.

4 egg whites
2 cups applesauce
1/2 tsp. lemon juice
1/8 tsp. ground cinnamon

Beat egg whites until stiff but not dry. Combine applesauce and lemon juice. Stir in 1 tbs. of egg whites, then fold in the rest. Spoon into individual cups and sprinkle with cinnamon. Serves 4.

per serving   70 calories, 3.8 g protein, 14.1 g carbo., 0.1 g fat, 14% calories from fat

YUMMY YOGURT

Here's a simple, healthy treat—a mix of yogurt, fruit, and cereal or trail mix.

1 cup plain yogurt, partially frozen
½ cup frozen fruit – strawberries, boysenberries, etc
¼ cup 100 sugar-free cereal or trail mix

Spoon yogurt into dish; add fruit and topping. Serves 2 to 3.

per serving   127 calories, 6.4 g protein, 10.5 g carbo., 7.2 g fat, 65 calories from fat

CHEESY POPOVERS

Add some extra protein by including cheese in your own popover recipe, or try this one.

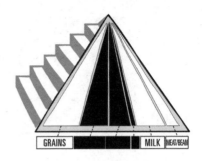

2 eggs
1 cup milk
1 cup flour
1/3 cup finely grated cheddar cheese

Beat eggs and milk until well blended. Add flour and cheese, and beat until smooth. Pour into 8 greased, preheated muffin tins and bake at 425° for 45 minutes. Makes 8.

per serving   107 calories, 5.2 g protein, 13.5 g carbo., 3.4 g fat, 31 calories from fat

MUNCHKINS

Tease little taste buds with bundles of fruit and nuts.

1$\frac{1}{2}$ cups boiling water
1 cup chopped dried apricots
$\frac{1}{4}$ cup raisins
$\frac{1}{2}$ cup chopped pecans
2 tbs. orange juice

In a bowl, pour boiling water over apricots and raisins and set aside for 30 minutes. Drain well. Mix in pecans and orange juice. Shape into balls and refrigerate. Makes 12 balls.

per ball   66 calories, 0.9 g protein, 10.1 g carbo., 3.1 g fat, 39% calories from fat

HOT NIBBLES

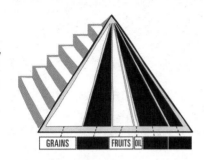

GRAINS   FRUITS OIL

Dried fruit and oats provide lots of carbohydrates and fiber. Fat can be minimized by reducing or omitting the sunflower kernels and the coconut.

1 tbs. reduced fat butter substitute (try 'Smart Balance' brand), melted
1/4 cup chopped dried apricots
1/4 cup raisins

1/4 cup sunflower kernels
1/4 cup unsweetened shredded coconut
1/4 cup chopped dates
1/4 cup rolled oats

Stir ingredients together in a skillet until heated through. Serve warm. Makes 6 servings.

per serving   133 calories, 2.7 g protein, 17.7 g carbo., 6.8 g fat, 43% calories from fat

SILLY SALAD

Three old favorites in a new setting.

VEGETABLES FRUITS MILK

1 cup grated carrots
¼ cup raisins
½ cup plain yogurt
1 can (8 oz. can) crushed pineapple, drained

Mix all ingredients and refrigerate until serving time. Serves 2.

per serving   170 calories, 4.9 g protein, 38.3 g carbo., 1.3 g fat, 12 calories from fat

FRUITY POPCORN

Serve this in small bowls, or form into balls.

GRAINS   FRUITS OIL   MEAT/BEAN

¹/₄ cup honey
¹/₄ cup water
¹/₄ cup reduced fat butter substitute
1 tbs. vanilla extract
¹/₂ tsp. salt
1 tsp. wheat germ
1 qt. air-popped popcorn

1 cup raisins
1 cup chopped dried apricots
1 cup sunflower kernels

Stir honey and water together over medium heat until a candy thermometer registers 250°. Add butter substitute, vanilla, salt and wheat germ. Pour over popcorn in a large bowl and mix well. Spread mixture into a large baking pan. Bake at 300° for 15 minutes. Remove from oven. Combine raisins, apricots and sunflower kernels. Stir in popcorn mixture. Place in pan and bake for 15 minutes longer. Cool. Serves 8.

per cup   282 calories, 5.9 g protein, 39.5 g carbo., 13.6 g fat, 40% calories from fat

DATE COOKIES

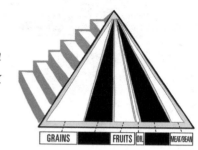

If you feel that jam and jelly are too high in sugar, try a pure fruit spread. Reduce the fat calories by cutting back on walnuts.

1 cup chopped dates
1 cup graham cracker crumbs
$\frac{1}{4}$ cup plum or strawberry jam
$\frac{1}{2}$ cup chopped walnuts
$\frac{1}{2}$ cup unsweetened shredded coconut

Combine dates, crumbs, jam and nuts. Drop by teaspoonfuls into a bowl of coconut and roll into balls. Cover and chill. Makes 24 cookies.

per cookie   63 calories, 0.7 g protein, 9.9 g carbo., 2.8 g fat, 37% calories from fat

PEANUT BUTTER MUFFINS

If they refuse to eat sandwiches, try this snack attack. Cut the fat calories further with nonfat (skim) milk and reduced fat peanut butter.

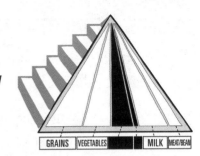

GRAINS | VEGETABLES | | MILK | MEAT/BEAN

1/3 cup brown sugar, firmly packed
1/3 cup peanut butter
1 egg
1/4 cup shredded carrots
3/4 cup flour
1/4 cup rolled oats

1 tsp. baking powder
1/4 tsp. baking soda
1/8 tsp. salt
1/2 cup 1% low-fat milk

Beat brown sugar and peanut butter; add egg and beat well. Stir in carrots. Add flour, oats, baking powder, soda, salt and milk, and beat until just blended. Pour into paper-lined muffin cups and bake at 400° for 15 to 20 minutes or until golden. Makes 8 to 10 muffins.

per muffin   168 calories, 5.6 g protein, 22.9 g carbo., 6.5 g fat, 34% calories from fat

JACK'S BEANSTALKS

Cheese and beans make a high-protein snack for after-school nibblers.

1 can (16 oz.) kidney beans
1/2 cup grated cheddar cheese
1/2 tsp. chili powder, if desired
8 celery stalks

Drain beans and save a little liquid. Mash beans with a fork, or process with a food processor or blender, adding a little bean liquid for a creamier texture. Stir in cheese and chili powder, if using. Simmer mixture in a small saucepan over low heat until cheese melts. Refrigerate. When cooled, stuff celery stalks with mixture. Cut into bite-sized pieces. Keep refrigerated in airtight containers. Makes 8 servings.

per serving   83 calories, 5 g protein, 10.5 g carbo., 2.6 g fat, 27% calories from fat

SPUMONI CELERY

Here's a trick way to cover the vegetable group. Try other combinations for variety.

1 carrot, finely chopped
1/4 cup finely chopped green bell pepper
1/2 cup low-fat cottage cheese
1/4 cup grated Parmesan cheese
6 celery stalks, cut into 3- to 4-inch pieces

Mix carrot, green pepper, cottage cheese and Parmesan together well. Stuff celery pieces. Makes 6 servings.

per serving   49 calories, 4.8 g protein, 3.8 g carbo., 1.7 g fat, 31% calories from fat

BANANA OATSIES

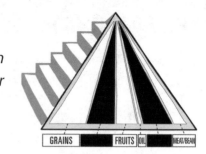

These fruit and cereal snacks are great to make when you're short on time. Cut the amount of walnuts to further reduce fat.

4 bananas
$1/2$ cup rolled oats
$3/4$ cup chopped walnuts
$3/4$ cup Grape Nuts cereal
1 tsp. vanilla extract

Mash bananas and add remaining ingredients. Mix well. Drop by teaspoonfuls onto an ungreased cookie sheet. Bake at 350° for 20 to 25 minutes. Makes 30 cookies.

per cookie   49 calories, 1.1 g protein, 7.4 g carbo., 2 g fat, 35% calories from fat

FRUIT COBBLER CRUNCH

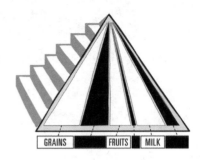

This is a quick and easy way to serve fruit. Use fruits canned in their own juice without added sugar.

1 can (8 oz.) peaches, pears, apricots or plums in juice
1 tsp. cinnamon
2 tbs. low-fat granola
2 tbs. plain (or fruit) low-fat yogurt

Drain fruit. Slice into 2 serving dishes. Sprinkle with cinnamon. Add granola and top with yogurt. Makes 2 servings.

per serving   101 calories, 1.9 g protein, 21.8 g carbo., 1.4 g fat, 12% calories from fat

PITA PARFAIT

How about a "fruit sandwich"?

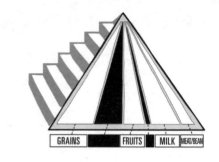

GRAINS   FRUITS   MILK   MEAT/BEAN

1 can (8 oz.) fruit cocktail, drained
2 tbs. low-fat cottage cheese
1 tbs. chopped almonds or walnuts
1 pita bread

Mix fruit with cottage cheese and nuts. Cut pita bread in half to make 2 pockets. Spoon fruit mixture into pita pockets. Makes 2 servings.

---

per serving   172 calories, 6.1 g protein, 31.2 g carbo., 3 g fat, 16% calories from fat

---

OVEN APPLES

These child-sized baked apples are perfect at breakfast, lunch, dinner or snack time.

4 small baking apples
2 tbs. chopped walnuts
2 tbs. raisins
1 tsp. cinnamon

Cut apples in half and hollow core. Place in a baking pan. Combine nuts, raisins and cinnamon in a small bowl. Stuff mixture into apple hollows. Cover and bake at 350° for 30 minutes. Serve warm, at room temperature or chilled. Makes 8 servings.

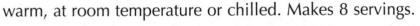

per serving   62 calories, 0.5 g protein, 13.2 g carbo., 1.4 g fat, 19% calories from fat

SUPER-HERO SNACKS

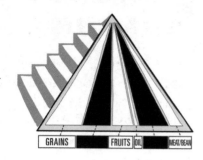

These provide lots of energy for ambitious youngsters. Reduce fat by using egg substitute instead of eggs. Eggs get about 60% of their calories from fat, while egg substitute, made mostly of egg whites, gets about 37% of its calories from fat. Use ¼ cup egg substitute for each large egg.

2 eggs
½ cup unsweetened applesauce
2 cups low-fat granola

Beat eggs well and blend into applesauce. Add granola and mix well. Spray an 8-inch square pan lightly with nonstick cooking spray. Press mixture firmly and evenly into pan. Bake at 350° for 20 minutes. Cut into bars and serve. Makes 9 bars.

per bar   134 calories, 4 g protein, 18.4 g carbo., 5.5 g fat, 37% calories from fat

APPLE SMACKS

Served warm or cold, these are always a favorite. Top them with yogurt if desired.

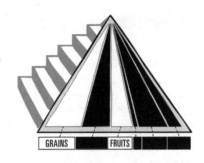

4 apples, sliced
¼ cup raisins
¼ cup water
¾ cup rolled oats
⅓ cup flour
¼ cup wheat germ

¼ cup butter substitute (try 'Smart Balance' brand)
2 tbs. honey, if desired
1 tsp. cinnamon

Spray an 8-inch square pan with nonstick cooking spray. Lay apple slices in pan. Combine remaining ingredients and sprinkle over apples. Bake at 350° for 35 minutes. Spoon into small dishes. Makes 4 servings.

per serving   365 calories, 5.7 g protein, 59.3 g carbo., 13.6 g fat, 32% calories from fat

YOGURT PLUS

Here's an easy way to cover the food pyramid in one delicious snack! The following are suggestions. Experiment with your own ideas. Use nuts and seeds sparingly, as they have naturally occurring fat.

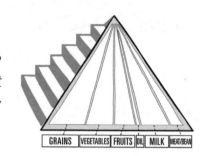

Start with 8 oz. plain (or vanilla) low-fat yogurt. Add one of the following from each group.

FRUITS

- sliced strawberries
- raspberries
- blueberries
- chopped apricots, fresh or dried
- chopped apples
- sliced bananas
- sectioned oranges
- raisins or other dried fruits
- chopped dates
- halved grapes
- sliced kiwi
- cubed melon
- sliced peaches
- diced pineapple

VEGETABLES

- shredded carrots
- diced celery
- chopped cucumber
- chopped red or yellow bell pepper
- diced tomato
- sliced jicama

NUTS AND SEEDS

- sunflower kernels
- sliced almonds
- sesame seeds
- reduced fat peanut butter
- chopped walnuts

GRAINS AND CEREALS

- cooked brown rice
- puffed rice
- Grape Nuts cereal
- low-fat granola
- whole wheat toast pieces
- wheat germ
- bran flakes
- crushed shredded wheat cereal

HOT CHEESE FUNNIES

This is a New York City special! Let the kids experiment by making up their own shapes. Decrease fat calories with reduced-fat or nonfat cheddar.

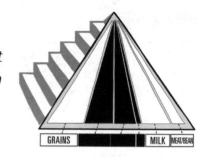

1 pkg. active dry yeast
1½ cups warm water (105° to 115°)
3½ cups flour
1 cup grated cheddar cheese
1 egg, beaten

Dissolve yeast in water. Stir in flour and cheese. Knead dough until smooth. (If the dough is too sticky, add more flour a teaspoon at a time.) Break off walnut-sized pieces and roll into 12-inch long ropes. Twist into pretzel shapes. Place shapes on an ungreased cookie sheet and brush with egg. Bake at 425° for 15 to 20 minutes. Serve warm. Makes about 30.

per pretzel   41 calories, 1.9 g protein, 4.9 g carbo., 1.5 g fat, 33% calories from fat

FRUIT CHEWIES

These snacks are high in fiber and naturally sweet. Reduce the amount of nuts, if desired, to lower the recipe's fat.

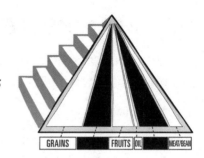

GRAINS FRUITS OIL MEAT/BEAN

3 bananas
1 cup chopped dates
¼ cup canola oil
2 cups rolled oats
½ cup chopped walnuts, peanuts or pecans
1 tsp. vanilla extract

Cut 2 of the bananas into medium-sized chunks. Mash 1 banana. Combine all ingredients and stir until mixed. Let stand for 10 minutes. Drop by teaspoonfuls onto a greased cookie sheet. Bake at 350° for 15 to 20 minutes. Makes 24 cookies.

per cookie   95 calories, 1.7 g protein, 13.8 g carbo., 4.3 g fat, 39% calories from fat

HAWAIIAN ROLLERS

Feed this energy-giving snack to a hungry soccer team. Since it's so quick and easy, why not double the recipe?

1 can (10 oz.) refrigerated pizza dough
$\frac{1}{2}$ cup pineapple preserves
$\frac{1}{2}$ tsp. cinnamon
$\frac{1}{4}$ cup unsweetened coconut
$\frac{1}{4}$ cup chopped walnuts

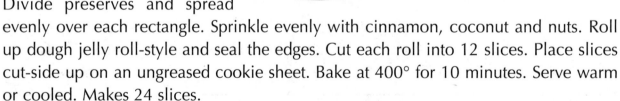

Cut dough into 2 rectangles. Divide preserves and spread evenly over each rectangle. Sprinkle evenly with cinnamon, coconut and nuts. Roll up dough jelly roll-style and seal the edges. Cut each roll into 12 slices. Place slices cut-side up on an ungreased cookie sheet. Bake at 400° for 10 minutes. Serve warm or cooled. Makes 24 slices.

per slice   45 calories, 1.3 g protein, 6.4 g carbo., 1.7 g fat, 35% calories from fat

BANANA BOMBS

These are great for outings and picnics.

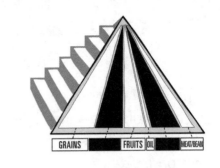

1 cup flour
$1/2$ tsp. baking soda
$1/2$ tsp. salt, if desired
$1/2$ cup chopped nuts or seeds
1 banana, cut into small chunks
$1/2$ cup chopped dates
1 egg
1 tsp. vanilla extract

Combine flour, soda, salt, if using, and nuts in a bowl. Combine banana, dates, egg and vanilla extract in a blender container. Blend until smooth. Add to dry ingredients and mix well. Drop by teaspoonfuls onto a greased cookie sheet. Flatten with the back of a spoon. Bake at 350° for 10 minutes. Makes 24 cookies.

per cookie   43 calories, 1.3 g protein, 5.8 g carbo., 1.8 g fat, 35% calories from fat

FLYING SAUCERS

Feed these to your little space-walkers.

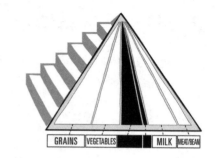

1 pkg. (10 oz.) refrigerated pizza dough
1 cup cooked ground turkey
1/2 cup grated Swiss cheese
1/2 cup frozen tiny peas, thawed
2 tbs. reduced fat mayonnaise
1 tbs. mustard

Cut dough into 8 equal pieces. Shape each piece into a ball, and flatten each ball to form a 4-inch disk. Combine remaining ingredients and divide among half of the disks. Top with remaining disks and seal edges closed with the tines of a fork. Bake at 375° for 15 to 20 minutes or until golden brown. Serve warm. Makes 4 servings.

per serving   325 calories, 18 g protein, 36.6 g carbo., 11.5 g fat, 32% calories from fat

MONKEY BARS

These cookie bars provide sustenance for playground antics.

$^1/_2$ cup reduced fat butter substitute
$^1/_4$ cup honey, or less if desired
1 egg

$^1/_4$ tsp. cinnamon

$^1/_2$ cup chopped prunes

1 banana, sliced

$^1/_2$ cup raisins

4 cups rolled oats

$^1/_2$ cup chopped walnuts

$^1/_2$ cup chopped dried apricots

$^1/_2$ cup sunflower kernels

Beat butter substitute and honey until light and fluffy. Add egg, cinnamon and bananas and beat well. Stir in remaining ingredients. Lightly spray a 9-x-13-inch pan with nonstick cooking spray. Spread mixture evenly into pan. Bake at 350° for 50 minutes. Cool and cut into bars. Makes 12 bars.

per bar   298 calories, 8 g protein, 39 g carbo., 14 g fat, 40% calories from fat

APPLENUTTIES

These cookies freeze well if they aren't all eaten first.

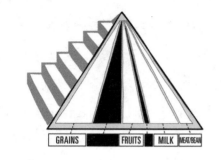

GRAINS FRUITS MILK MEAT/BEAN

1 cup apple butter
$^{1}/_{2}$ cup peanut butter
1 tsp. vanilla extract
$^{3}/_{4}$ cup instant nonfat dry milk
$^{3}/_{4}$ cup flour
$^{1}/_{4}$ tsp. cinnamon
$^{1}/_{2}$ cup raisins

Beat apple butter, peanut butter and vanilla together in a bowl. Add dry milk, flour, cinnamon and raisins. Mix well. Drop by teaspoonfuls onto a greased cookie sheet. Flatten with the tines of a fork. Bake at 350° for 10 minutes. Serve warm or chilled. Makes 30 cookies.

per cookie   68 calories, 2.1 g protein, 10.5 g carbo., 2.3 g fat, 29% calories from fat

BAKED VEGGIE SPREAD

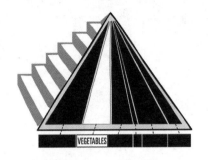

Serve this spread cold with toasted bread or rye crackers. It's a sneaky way to get kids to eat their veggies.

1 eggplant, unpeeled
2 carrots
1 pkg. (10 oz.) French-cut green beans
3 small zucchini
3/4 cup ketchup
1 can (8 oz.) tomato sauce
1 tbs. olive oil

Chop eggplant, carrots, beans and zucchini and place in a baking dish. Combine ketchup, tomato sauce and oil. Pour over veggies. Bake, covered, at 325° for 1 1/2 hours. Serve cold. Makes 6 cups.

per 1/2 cup   50 calories, 1.3 g protein, 9.7 g carbo., 1.3 g fat, 21% calories from fat

ZIPPETY DIPS

Dips are a great way for kids to eat vegetables, fruit and other nutritious foods. Unless otherwise stated, veggie dippers can be raw or cooked. Raw vegetables have more nutrients than their cooked counterparts.

VEGGIE DIPPERS

- cooked artichokes
- asparagus spears
- cooked baby red potatoes
- broccoli florets
- carrot sticks
- cauliflower florets
- celery sticks
- cherry tomatoes
- cucumber rounds
- fennel strips
- raw mushrooms
- bell pepper strips
- jicama slices
- pickles
- radishes
- cooked turnip strips
- yam or sweet potato strips
- yellow squash slices
- zucchini strips

FRUIT DIPPERS

- apple wedges
- bananas
- melon slices
- grapes
- Mandarin orange segments
- melon slices
- pear wedges
- pineapple slices
- strawberries

OTHER DIPPERS

- breadsticks
- chicken strips
- gingersnaps
- low salt tortilla chips
- whole wheat crackers
- crispy pita wedges
- toasted French bread rounds
- toast shapes
- pretzels
- cooked shrimp
- canned water chestnuts

CHILI DIP

Kidney beans are a good source of vitamin A, protein and fiber.

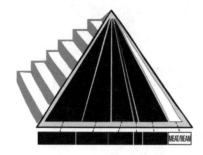

1 can (16 oz.) kidney beans, drained
1 tbs. vinegar
3/4 tsp. chili powder

1/4 tsp. salt
1 tbs. minced onion
1 tsp. dried parsley

Combine ingredients in a blender container; whirl until smooth. Makes 1 1/2 cups.

COTTAGE CHEESE DIP

This calcium-rich dip will appeal to even the most die-hard milk hater.

1 cup plain nonfat yogurt
1 cup low-fat cottage cheese
1/4 cup grated Parmesan cheese
1/4 cup canned artichoke hearts, drained

Combine ingredients in a blender container; whirl until smooth. Makes 2 1/2 cups.

FRUIT DIP

This dip makes a good milkshake when blended with a little cold nonfat (skim) milk. Use the kids' favorite fruit.

1 cup plain nonfat yogurt   1/2 cup chopped fruit

Combine ingredients in a blender container; whirl until smooth. Makes 1 1/2 cups.

DYNAMITE DRINKS

47 Four-Fruit Float	**59** Boysenberry Blitz
48 Monkey Milkshake	**59** Boysenberry Milkshake
49 V-3 Juice	**60** Fruit Frappé
50 Simple Simon Cider	**61** Blender Berries
51 Fruit Juicie	**62** Peach Fuzz
52 Graham Cracker Foamy	**63** Breakfast Shake
53 Surprise Wheat Germ Shake	**64** Apple Shake
54 Mighty Milk	**64** Frosty Fruit Float
55 Fruity Lemonade	**65** Hawaiian Shake
56 Jersey Juice	**66** Banana Smoothy
56 Mooseberry Juice	**67** Banana Chocolate Froth
57 Orange Jubilee	**68** Grape Slush
58 New York "Egg Cream"	**69** Bananorangberry Smoothie

FOUR-FRUIT FLOAT

So refreshing! Use fresh or frozen berries

½ cup sliced strawberries
½ cup raspberries
½ cup blueberries
½ cup 1% low-fat milk
1 cup apple juice

Combine ingredients in a blender container. Blend until smooth. Makes 2 to 4 servings.

---

per serving   67 calories, 1.4 g protein, 14.4 g carbo., 0.9 g fat, 11% calories from fat

---

MONKEY MILKSHAKE

This is a meal in a glass. Even those who don't like milk will ask for more.

1 cup sliced strawberries
1 banana
1 cup nonfat (skim) milk
2 tsp. vanilla extract
3 ice cubes

Combine ingredients in a blender container. Blend until smooth and fluffy. Makes 2 to 3 servings.

per serving   117 calories, 5.2 g protein, 24.6 g carbo., 0.8 g fat, 5% calories from fat

V-3 JUICE

It's worth a try, isn't it? If the kids don't go for this, you'll be happy to drink it yourself.

¹/₄ cup chopped celery
¹/₄ cup coarsely grated peeled carrot
¹/₄ cup any other vegetable
1 cup tomato juice

Combine ingredients in a blender container. Blend until smooth. Serve immediately or chill before serving. Makes 2 servings.

per serving   35 calories, 1.3 g protein, 8.5 g carbo., 0.1 g fat, 3% calories from fat

SIMPLE SIMON CIDER

Perfect for a cold winter evening or in the lunch box vacuum bottle.

3 cinnamon sticks
1 bottle (46 oz.) natural apple juice
1 can (11.5 oz.) apricot nectar

Bring ingredients to a boil in a large saucepan. Simmer for 10 minutes. Serve warm. Makes 6 to 8 servings.

per serving   133 calories, 0.3 g protein, 33.6 g carbo., 0.3 g fat, 2% calories from fat

FRUIT JUICIE

Makes enough for the whole neighborhood.

1 pint strawberries
2 tbs. lemon juice
3 cups boiling water
3 cups cold water
½ cup orange juice
crushed ice

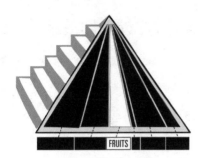

Combine ½ of the strawberries, lemon juice and boiling water in a blender container. Blend until smooth. Pour into a large bowl or pitcher. Repeat process with remaining strawberries, lemon juice and boiling water and add to first mixture. Stir in cold water and orange juice. Chill. Serve over crushed ice. Makes 8 to 10 servings.

per serving   25 calories, 0.5 g protein, 5.9 g carbo., 0.3 g fat, 8% calories from fat

GRAHAM CRACKER FOAMY

This makes a good breakfast drink.

1½ cups 1% low-fat milk
2 graham crackers, broken
½ tsp. honey, if desired
2 tbs. frozen orange juice concentrate

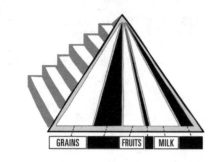

Combine ingredients in a blender container. Blend until smooth and frothy. Makes 2 servings.

per serving   152 calories, 7.1 g protein, 22.2 g carbo., 4.2 g fat, 24% calories from fat

SURPRISE WHEAT GERM SHAKE

You can't taste the wheat germ, yet it adds so much!

6 tbs. frozen orange juice concentrate
1 cup 1% low-fat milk
2 tsp. wheat germ
3 ice cubes

Combine ingredients in a blender container. Blend until frothy. Makes 2 servings.

per serving   153 calories, 5.8 g protein, 27.3 g carbo., 2.7 g fat, 15% calories from fat

MIGHTY MILK

Buttermilk, despite its name, does not contain any but-ter. It's actually 1% low-fat milk with the addition of bene-ficial bacteria as you would find in yogurt. Although it has a slightly sour taste that many kids don't like, this recipe disguises it. Honestly, you can't taste the buttermilk.

1 can (6 oz.) frozen orange juice concentrate
2 cups buttermilk
1 tsp. honey

Combine ingredients in a blender container. Blend until frothy. Serve over ice. Makes 2 to 4 servings.

per serving   245 calories, 10.2 g protein, 47.1 g carbo., 2.3 g fat, 8% calories from fat

FRUITY LEMONADE

You can substitute 1 qt. lemonade made from frozen concentrate for the first 3 ingredients if you prefer. Use raspberries, blackberries, boysenberries and/or chopped strawberries.

2 large lemons
1/2 cup honey, or to taste
3 1/2 cups water
1 cup fresh berries or thawed frozen
  berries

Squeeze lemons through a strainer into a large bowl. Stir in honey gradually to taste. Add water and berries. Pour into glasses and serve. Makes 4 to 6 servings.

per serving   148 calories, 0.7 g protein, 40 g carbo., 0.2 g fat, 1% calories from fat

JERSEY JUICE

Juice and milk? It's surprisingly good!

1 can (6 oz.) frozen orange juice
concentrate

2½ cups 1% low-fat milk

Combine ingredients in a blender container. Blend until frothy. Makes 3 servings.

per serving   191 calories, 8.1 g protein, 30.4 g carbo., 4 g fat, 19% calories from fat

MOOSEBERRY JUICE

Sneak in a little wheat germ any time you can!

1 pkg. (10 oz.) frozen raspberries
1½ cups 1% low-fat milk

1 tbs. wheat germ

Combine ingredients in a blender container. Blend until smooth. Makes 3 servings.

per serving   165 calories, 5.2 g protein, 31.6 g carbo., 2.7 g fat, 14% calories from fat

ORANGE JUBILEE

Make plain orange juice elegant and extra-nutritious. Add a little water if the blender won't turn.

1 can (6 oz.) orange juice concentrate
1/3 cup instant nonfat dry milk
1/2 tsp. vanilla extract
ice cubes to fill blender

Place orange juice concentrate into a blender container. Add instant milk and blend until mixed. Add vanilla extract and ice cubes and blend on high speed until smooth. Makes 2 servings.

per serving   176 calories, 6 g protein, 38.4 g carbo., 0.3 fat, 1% calories from fat

NEW YORK "EGG CREAM"

*Only in New York would a drink called Egg Cream be make without eggs or cream. A legend! Serve with **Hot Cheese Funnies**, page 34. The carob is a great and healthier substitute for chocolate.*

1 cup club soda
1 cup 1% low-fat milk
1 tsp. carob powder
1 tsp. honey

Combine ingredients in a blender container. Blend on high speed until frothy. Makes 2 servings.

per serving   81 calories, 4.2 g protein, 11.4 g carbo., 2.4 g fat, 26% calories from fat

BOYSENBERRY BLITZ

This is very refreshing on a warm day. Serve in frosty glasses.

1 cup 1% low-fat milk
1 carton (8 oz.) boysenberry low-fat yogurt

Combine ingredients in a blender container. Blend until frothy. Makes 2 servings.

per serving   176 calories, 9 g protein, 27.5 g carbo., 3.6 g fat, 18% calories from fat

VARIATION: BOYSENBERRY MILKSHAKE

Combine 1 cup frozen boysenberries, 1 cup low-fat vanilla ice cream and ¼ cup 1% low-fat milk in a blender container. Blend until smooth. Makes 2 servings.

per serving   135 calories, 4.4 g protein, 24 g carbo., 3 g fat, 19% calories from fat

FRUIT FRAPPE

Use berries, peaches, apricots, pears or melon for this Italian favorite.

²/₃ cup 1% low-fat milk
²/₃ cup fresh fruit, cut into pieces
1 tsp. honey, if desired
¹/₄ cup crushed ice

Combine ingredients in a blender container. Blend on high speed until smooth and frothy. Makes 2 servings.

per serving   70 calories, 3 g protein, 11.6 g carbo., 1.6 g fat, 20% calories from fat

BLENDER BERRIES

Choose your favorite: strawberries, blueberries or boy-senberries.

1/2 cup plain nonfat yogurt
2 tbs. water
1 cup fresh or frozen berries
1 banana
1 tbs. wheat germ
1/8 tsp. cinnamon
1/4 tsp. lemon juice

Combine ingredients in a blender container. Blend until smooth. Serve chilled in frosty glasses. Makes 2 servings.

per serving   126 calories, 4.6 g protein, 25.6 g carbo., 1.6 g fat, 10% calories from fat

PEACH FUZZ

Many of the canned fruits today are available without added sugar. Look for labels that say "lite," "natural," or "packed in its own juice." Some have added no extra sugar and others have reduce the amount by 50%. You can substitute 2 peeled ripe peaches for canned peaches when they're are in season.

1 banana
3 canned peach halves
2 cups 1% low-fat milk

½ tsp. vanilla extract
1 carton (8 oz.) plain low-fat yogurt
5 ice cubes

Combine all ingredients in a blender container. Blend until smooth and frothy. Makes 4 to 6 servings.

per serving   564 calories, 7.6 g protein, 21.4 g carbo., 3.4 g fat, 21% calories from fat

BREAKFAST SHAKE

No time to cook breakfast? Try this as a morning meal with some whole grain toast.

2 cups nonfat (skim) milk
1/2 cup plain low-fat yogurt
1 tbs. vanilla extract
2 tsp. nutmeg
1 cup instant nonfat dry milk
1 banana
1 can (6 oz.) frozen orange juice concentrate

Place all ingredients in a blender container. Blend until frothy. Makes 4 servings.

per serving   221 calories, 13 g protein, 40.3 g carbo., 1.4 g fat, 6% calories from fat

APPLE SHAKE

Substitute different fruit juices for variety.

1 cup low-fat vanilla ice cream $1/4$ tsp. cinnamon
$1/2$ cup apple juice

Place ingredients in a blender container. Blend until smooth and frothy. Serves 2.

per serving   121 calories, 2.6 g protein, 22 g carbo., 2.9 g fat, 21% calories from fat

FROSTY FRUIT FLOAT

Use orange, grape, cranberry, pineapple or any other favorite fruit juice.

$1/4$ cup fruit juice   1 bottle (10 oz.) club soda
1 tbs. low-fat vanilla ice cream

Pour juice into a glass. Add ice cream. Fill with club soda. Stir and serve. Serves 2.

per serving   19 calories, 0.4 g protein, 4 g carbo., 0.3 g fat, 12% calories from fat

HAWAIIAN SHAKE

Substitute fresh pineapple for the canned variety when you find it in the market. Process it for a few seconds in a food processor or blender to "crush."

2 cups crushed pineapple
2 cups nonfat (skim) milk
1 pint low-fat vanilla ice cream
1 tbs. lemon juice

Combine ingredients in a blender container. Blend until smooth. Makes 6 to 8 servings.

per serving   153 calories, 4.8 g protein, 26.8 g carbo., 3.5 g fat, 20% calories from fat

BANANA SMOOTHY

Make a bet with your child that she or he can drink a whole banana.

1½ cups 1% low-fat milk
1 large banana
¼ tsp. vanilla extract
¼ cup low-fat vanilla ice cream

Combine ingredients in a blender container. Blend until smooth and creamy. Makes 2 servings.

per serving   166 calories, 7.4 g protein, 25.6 g carbo., 4.5 g fat, 23% calories from fat

BANANA CHOCOLATE FROTH

This potassium-packed shake tastes deceptively rich.

1 cup 1% low-fat milk
1 banana
3/4 cup low-fat vanilla ice cream
2 tbs. cocoa powder

Combine ingredients in a blender container. Blend until smooth and creamy. Makes 2 servings.

per serving   188 calories, 7.1 g protein, 31.4 g carbo., 5.2 g fat, 23% calories from fat

GRAPE SLUSH

This shake tastes like liquid sherbet; a favorite!

¼ cup frozen grape juice concentrate
¼ cup frozen orange juice concentrate
½ cup 1% low-fat milk
½ cup low-fat vanilla ice cream
1 banana

FRUITS   MILK

Combine all ingredients in a blender container. Blend until smooth. Serve in icy cold glasses. Makes 2 servings.

per serving   249 calories, 5 g protein, 53 g carbo., 3 g fat, 11% calories from fat

BANANORANGBERRY SMOOTHIE

This thick drink gives your child a head start on the food pyramid's fruit group. Garnish glasses with an orange slice and a crazy curly straw.

1 cup strawberries
1 banana
1 cup orange juice

Place all ingredients in a blender container and process until smooth. Makes 2 to 3 servings.

per serving 130 calories, 1.9 g protein, 31.5 g carbo., 0.8 g fat, 5% calories from fat

FROZEN FUN

71 Put Your Local Ice Cream Truck Out of Business

72 Banana Push-Ups

73 Frozen Bananas

74 Eskimo Fruit

75 King Kong's Chips

76 Frostbite Blizzard

77 Wiggle Sicles

78 Banana Frostee

79 Banana Pineapple Bars

80 Tropical Pops

81 Arctic Oranges

82 Hawaiian Ice

83 Frozen Jammies

84 Fruit Sherbies

85 Gellapops

86 Chocksicles

87 Rabbit Sherbet

88 Cinnamon Sicles

89 Frozen Yoggies

90 Hula Pops

91 Peacheritos

92 Freeze Your Favorites

93 Iced Teasers

94 Watermelon Wannabes

PUT YOUR LOCAL ICE CREAM TRUCK OUT OF BUSINESS

Frozen snacks are extremely popular with kids all year long. They are a great way to disguise unpopular fruits and vegetables. (Your child doesn't have to know how Rabbit Sherbet got its name.) Sugar should be kept to a minimum in a child's diet, but it doesn't have to be avoided altogether. A little jam for flavor, or sherbet or low-fat ice cream, combined with other nutritious ingredients, can become a special frozen treat that most children are sure to eat.

The main object of all the recipes in this book is to help you make your child's diet as healthy as possible. Since snacks are a big part of that diet, they are a great vehicle for packing healthy foods into favorites a child will eat. The snacks in this chapter are easy to make, taste great and are a lot more nutritious than the frozen "colored sugar water" you can buy at the supermarket. They are probably a lot less expensive, too.

If you don't have popsicle molds, keep on hand a supply of popsicle sticks, empty juice cans and 5 or 9 oz. paper "dixie" cups to make homemade popsicles. If using cans, dip them briefly in hot water to loosen the frozen snack. Paper cups can simply be peeled away and discarded.

BANANA PUSH-UPS

Kids enjoy pushing these pops up from the cup.

2 bananas, cut up
$1/2$ cup instant nonfat dry milk
1 cup plain or banana yogurt
1 can (6 oz.) frozen orange juice concentrate
1 cup water

Combine all ingredients in blender and whirl until foamy. Pour into paper cups and freeze. Push up from bottom of cup. Serves 6.

per serving   106 calories, 3.3 g protein, 23.7 g carbo., 0.8 g fat, 8 calories from fat

FROZEN BANANAS

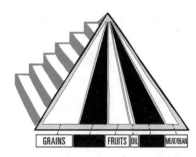

Serve these on a high activity day for a quick energy boost. Reduced fat peanut butter can be used to lower the fat percentage. Cut these into small chips for the young ones.

2 bananas
1/2 cup peanut butter
1/2 cup wheat germ

Peel bananas and cut in half crosswise. Insert a popsicle stick into the flat end of each banana. Wrap bananas in plastic wrap and freeze. When frozen, place peanut butter and wheat germ into separate bowls. Dip bananas into peanut butter and then into wheat germ and serve. Makes 4 servings.

per serving   291 calories, 10.1 g protein, 31.6 g carbo., 16.3 g fat, 47% calories from fat

ESKIMO FRUIT

Sometimes just making it cold makes fruit taste better! Put one or more of the following items in the freezer for a refreshing treat. Or, make up your own frozen fun.

- apples
- apricots
- bananas
- blueberries
- cantaloupe
- cherries
- dried fruits
- fruit leather
- gelatin snacks
- grapefruit
- grapes
- kiwi
- mangoes
- oranges
- papayas
- peaches
- pineapple
- plums
- raisins
- raspberries
- strawberries
- watermelon

KING KONG'S CHIPS

These treats take only minutes and the kids can help.

2 bananas, sliced
1/2 cup orange juice
1/2 cup wheat germ

Dip banana slices into orange juice then into wheat germ. Arrange in cake pans or on plates in a single layer. Cover with plastic and freeze. Makes 4 servings.

per serving   111 calories, 3.7 g protein, 23 g carbo., 1.6 g fat, 12% calories from fat

FROSTBITE BLIZZARD

The kids will think they've gone to the fair for snow cones, but their lips won't be stained blue.

ice cubes
fruit nectar, fruit juice or fruit puree

Crush ice in a heavy plastic bag with a hammer or use a blender or food processor to make "snow." Scoop into a bowl. Pour fruit juice or puree over snow and serve with a spoon.

per cup fruit nectar   140 calories, 0.9 g protein, 36.1 g carbo., 0 g fat, 0% calories from fat

WIGGLE SICLES

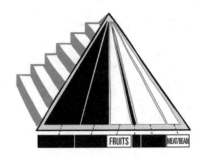

You can substitute packaged gelatin or pudding for unflavored gelatin and fruit puree, but those products are high in refined sugar. the protein in this recipe comes from the gelatin.

1 pkg. (1/4 oz.) unflavored gelatin
3/4 cup boiling water
1/2 cup fruit puree (strawberry, plum, peach, etc.)

Dissolve gelatin in boiling water. Add fruit puree. Stir until well blended and pour into paper cups. Cover cups with foil. Make a slit in the center of each foil cover. Insert sticks and freeze. Makes 2 servings.

per serving   45 calories, 3.2 g protein, 8.7 g carbo., 0 g fat, 0% calories from fat

BANANA FROSTEE

Vanilla extract is the secret ingredient in this recipe. It adds an extra flavor dimension that your kids will love.

1/4 cup apple juice
2 bananas, sliced and frozen
1 tsp. vanilla extract
1/2 cup chilled sliced peaches or strawberries

Combine juice and bananas in a blender container. Blend until creamy. Quickly blend in chilled fruit. Serve immediately. Makes 2 servings.

per serving   130 calories, 1.4 g protein, 33 g carbo., 0.7 g fat, 4% calories from fat

BANANA-PINEAPPLE BARS

Here's a popsicle with the taste of the tropics.

1 cup pineapple juice
1 banana

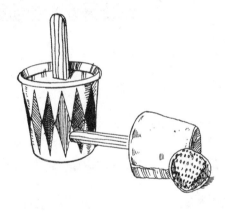

Combine juice and banana in a blender container. Blend on high speed until smooth. Pour into paper cups. Cover cups with foil. Make a slit in the center of each foil cover. Insert popsicle sticks. Freeze. Makes 2 servings.

per serving   117 calories, 1.1 g protein, 29.3 g carbo., 0.3 g fat, 2% calories from fat

TROPICAL POPS

Ask the kids to guess what flavor these are. Odds are they won't figure it out.

1 apple, peeled and chopped
1 orange, peeled and sectioned
1 banana, peeled and sliced
1/2 cup sliced pineapple, fresh or canned
1 pear, peeled and chopped
1 cup frozen strawberries with juice

Combine all ingredients in a blender container and puree. Pour into paper cups. Cover cups with foil. Make a slit in the center of each foil cover. Insert popsicle sticks and freeze. Makes 4 to 6 servings.

per serving   109 calories, 1.1 g protein, 27.8 g carbo., 0.6 g fat, 4% calories from fat

ARCTIC ORANGES

Save these for a special occasion. Garnish with a little yogurt and a cherry. Mom: add 3 tbs. Grand Marnier to the mixture and serve them at your next dinner party!

3 oranges
¼ cup honey, or to taste
½ cup water
1 tbs. lemon juice

Using a zigzag pattern, cut tops off oranges. Hollow out and reserve fruit. Set orange shells in muffin cups so they won't topple over. Squeeze and strain orange juice. Set aside. Cook honey and water in a small saucepan over low heat until slightly thickened, about 15 minutes. Add orange juice and lemon juice to mixture. Fill oranges and freeze. Makes 6 servings.

per serving   74 calories, 0.7 g protein, 19.5 g carbo., 0.1 g fat, 1% calories from fat

HAWAIIAN ICE

Peaches can be substituted for nectarines.

4 nectarines, cubed
2 bananas, sliced
juice of 2 oranges
juice of 2 lemons
1 can (8 oz.) crushed pineapple
1/2 cup water

Combine nectarines and bananas in a blender container. Blend until smooth. Add orange juice, lemon juice, pineapple and water. Blend until smooth. Pour into a large container. Cover and freeze. When ready to serve, let stand at room temperature for about 20 minutes. Scoop into individual dishes. Makes 6 to 8 servings.

per serving   128 calories, 2 g protein, 32.5 g carbo., 0.7 g fat, 5% calories from fat

FROZEN JAMMIES

Combining these unusual ingredients yields a surprisingly delicious frozen treat.

3 cups buttermilk
2 cups strawberry or plum jam

Beat ingredients together until blended. Pour into ice cube trays and freeze until firm. Release cubes from tray and beat with an electric mixer until fluffy. Spoon into individual containers and return to freezer until ready to serve. Makes 4 to 6 servings.

per serving   510 calories, 7.1 g protein, 120.8 g carbo., 1.8 g fat, 3% calories from fat

FRUIT SHERBIES

Don't mention the word buttermilk and they'll ask for more.

1 can (6 oz.) frozen orange juice concentrate
3 cans water
2 cups fruit puree or nectar
²/₃ cup buttermilk

Combine ingredients. Pour into paper cups. Cover cups with foil. Make a small slit in the center of each cover. Insert popsicle sticks and freeze. Makes 4 to 6 servings.

per serving   151 calories, 2.7 g protein, 35.5 g carbo., 0.5 g fat, 3% calories from fat

GELLAPOPS

These are much more nutritious than commercial popsicles. Apple or grape juice concentrate make nice variations. Gelatin adds protein to these jiggly popsicles.

1½ pkg. (¼ oz. each) unflavored gelatin
¾ cup boiling water
1 can (6 oz.) frozen orange juice concentrate
2 cups cold water
1 carton (32 oz.) plain low-fat yogurt

Dissolve gelatin in boiling water in a large bowl. Add juice concentrate and cold water. Add yogurt and stir until blended. Pour into paper cups. Cover cups with foil. Make a small slit in the center of each foil cover. Insert popsicle sticks and freeze. Makes 6 to 8 servings.

per serving   146 calories, 10.1 g protein, 21.5 g carbo., 2.4 g fat, 15% calories from fat

CHOCKSICLES

Appease your chocolate lovers with this low-fat treat.

1 cup plain low-fat yogurt
2 tbs. cocoa powder
1 tsp. honey

Blend ingredients and pour into paper cups. Cover cups with foil. Make a small slit in the center of each foil cover. Insert sticks and freeze. Makes 2 servings.

per serving   96 calories, 6.9 g protein, 13.5 g carbo., 2.8 g fat, 23% calories from fat

RABBIT SHERBET

This snack is devious, but delicious. Carrots are an important source of vitamins.

1 cup sliced cooked carrots
¼ cup orange juice
1 pint orange sherbet, softened

Combine carrots and orange juice in a blender container. Blend until smooth. Fold into softened sherbet. Pour into a large plastic container or bowl. Cover and freeze. Scoop sherbet into individual cups to serve. Makes 3 to 4 servings.

per serving   205 calories, 2 g protein, 45 g carbo., 2.7 g fat, 11% calories from fat

CINNAMON SICLES

Eating these is just like eating frozen apple pies.

1 cup plain low-fat yogurt
1 cup applesauce
1/2 tsp. cinnamon
1 tbs. honey, if desired

Blend yogurt, applesauce, cinnamon and honey, if using. Pour into paper cups. Cover cups with foil. Make a slit in the center of each foil cover and insert popsicle sticks. Freeze. Makes 2 to 3 servings.

per serving   157 calories, 6.2 g protein, 30.9 g carbo., 1.8 g fat, 10% calories from fat

FROZEN YOGGIES

It is possible to make your own frozen yogurt pops, and yours won't have additives or preservatives.

1 cup orange juice
2 cups plain low-fat yogurt
1 tsp. vanilla extract

Combine juice, yogurt and vanilla extract. Pour into paper cups. Cover cups with foil. Make a slit in the center of each foil cover and insert popsicle sticks. Freeze until firm. Makes 3 to 4 servings.

per serving   133 calories, 8.5 g protein, 19.6 g carbo., 2.4 g fat, 16% calories from fat.

HULA POPS

These taste perfect after a long day at the beach. Use apricots, strawberries, peaches, nectarines, pineapple or a combination for the fruit.

1 cup plain low-fat yogurt
1 banana
1 tsp. honey, if desired
½ cup orange or pineapple juice
1 cup sliced fruit

Combine ingredients in a blender container. Blend on high speed until smooth. Pour into paper cups. Cover cups with foil. Make a slit in the center of each foil cover. Insert sticks and freeze. Makes 6 to 8 servings.

per serving   61 calories, 2.5 g protein, 11.9 g carbo., 0.8 g fat, 11% calories from fat

PEACHERITOS

Experiment with strawberries or bananas too.

1 can (28 oz.) peaches or 3 fresh peaches, peeled and
  sliced
1½ cups 1% low-fat milk

Combine ingredients in a blender container. Blend until smooth. Pour into paper cups. Cover cups with foil. Make a small slit in the center of each foil cover. Insert popsicle sticks and freeze. Makes 4 to 6 servings.

per serving   74 calories, 3.5 g protein, 11.6 g carbo., 1.8 g fat, 21% calories from fat

FREEZE YOUR FAVORITES

*Almost anything tastes better to kids when it is frozen. Pour your child's favorite drink into popsicle molds and watch his or her face light up with excitement. Choose any of the following drinks from the **Dynamite Drinks** chapter or make up your own recipe.*

- *Four-Fruit Float*, page 47
- *Fruit Juicie*, page 51
- *Mighty Milk*, page 54
- *Fruity Lemonade*, page 55
- *Jersey Juice*, page 56
- *New York "Egg Cream,"* page 58

- *Boysenberry Blitz*, page 59
- *Boysenberry Milkshake*, page 59
- *Breakfast Shake*, page 63
- *Hawaiian Shake*, page 65
- *Banana Smoothie*, page 66
- *Bananorangberry Smoothie*, page 69

ICE TEASERS

Herbal tea is refreshing and light to drink on a hot summer day, but it's even more fun frozen. Toss bits of fruit into the popsicle cup for garnish.

3 cups brewed herbal tea, such as lemon or berry
3 cups orange juice

Blend ingredients. Pour into paper cups or popsicle molds. Cover cups with foil. Make a small slit in the center of each foil cover. Insert popsicle sticks and freeze. Makes 6 to 8 servings.

per serving   57 calories, 0.9 g protein, 13.1 g carbo., 0.3 g fat, 4% calories from fat

WATERMELON WANNABES

Watermelon in rich in vitamins A and C, and kids love it. The carob chips resemble seeds, but they taste better.

2 cups chopped seeded watermelon
1 cup apple juice
$1/2$ cup carob chips

Combine watermelon and apple juice in a blender container. Blend until smooth. Pour into a freezer-proof bowl and freeze until semi-solid. Stir in carob chips. Carefully spoon mixture into paper cups. Cover cups with foil. Make a small slit in the center of each foil cover. Insert popsicle sticks and freeze until solid. Makes 6 to 8 servings.

per serving   83 calories, 0.4 g protein, 13.8 g carbo., 2.4 g fat, 29% calories from fat

BETTER BREAKFASTS

96 Baked Banana Bars
97 Frisky Frittata
98 Hot Cereal Surprise
99 Macaroni Omelet
100 Nutty Fruit Toast
101 Square Meal Squares
102 Sweet Bread
103 Cheesy Breakfast Sandwich
104 Fruit-n-Cheese Toast
105 Coconut Toasties
106 Make-Believe Waffles

107 Banana Francais
108 Instant Brunch
109 Potpourri Waffles
110 Funny Face Pancakes
111 Picky Eater Zucchini Pancakes
112 Tasty Toppings
113 Fruit-n-Cereal Squares
114 Breakfast Bars
115 Easy Cinnamon Rolls
116 Breakfast Banana Split

It is recommended that children over the age of 2 eat no more than 30% of their daily calories in the form of fat. Also, remember that the guidelines are for TOTAL DAILY CALORIES. It's OK to indulge at one meal as long as you moderate fat intake throughout the day.

BAKED BANANA BARS

Try this dip-and-bake breakfast.

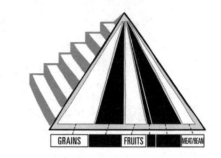

GRAINS   FRUITS   MEAT/BEAN

4 bananas
1 egg
2 tbs. orange juice
2 cups bran flakes or crisp rice cereal

Peel bananas, cut in half, and insert a popsicle stick in one end of each half. Crack egg into small bowl and add orange juice; beat with a fork. Put bran flakes in a small bowl and crush with a fork. Dip each banana in liquid, then roll in flakes to coat. Place on a cookie sheet and bake at 375° for 10 minutes. Let cool for 10 minutes before serving. Makes 8.

per serving   88 calories, 1.8 g protein, 20.0 g carbo., 0.8 g fat, 7 calories from fat

FRISKY FRITTATA

Half pizza, half quiche, but all delicious!

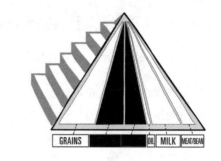

1 egg
³/₄ cup flour
¹/₂ tsp. salt
¹/₄ tsp. dried oregano
1 cup 1% low-fat milk
1 cup grated part-skim mozzarella cheese
3 tbs. grated Parmesan cheese

Mix egg with flour, salt, oregano and milk. Pour into a blender container and whirl until foamy. Add mozzarella cheese and pour into a greased pie pan. Bake at 400° for 30 minutes. Top with Parmesan cheese. Broil briefly until Parmesan is slightly melted. Serve warm or cold. Makes 6 servings.

per serving   157 calories, 10.5 g protein, 14.7 g carbo., 5.9 g fat, 35% calories from fat

HOT CEREAL SURPRISE

Mikey won't eat his Maypo? Try this little surprise.

1 cup cooked oatmeal
1 apple, chopped
1 cup 1% low-fat milk
1-2 tbs. honey, if desired
1/4 cup raisins, chopped dried apricots or dates
1/4 tsp. cinnamon

Combine cooked cereal, apple, milk, honey, if using, fruit and cinnamon in a saucepan. Cook over low heat for 5 to 10 minutes. Serve hot. Makes 2 servings.

per serving   277 calories, 7.9 g protein, 56.5 g carbo., 3.9 g fat, 12% calories from fat

MACARONI OMELET

By using egg substitute instead of eggs, you can reduce the fat in this recipe from 41% to 31%. Use 1/4 cup liquid egg substitute for each large egg. Serve this omelet in scooped-out orange halves for a fresh look.

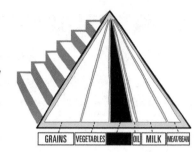

2 eggs, beaten
1 cup chopped cooked broccoli
1/2 cup cooked macaroni
1/4 cup grated Parmesan cheese

Mix eggs with broccoli and macaroni. Scramble in a nonstick skillet until fluffy. Sprinkle with Parmesan cheese. Makes 2 servings.

per serving   203 calories, 15.5 g protein, 15 g carbo., 9.3 g fat, 41% calories from fat

NUTTY FRUITY TOAST

This recipe puts a whole breakfast on a slice of toast. If desired, substitute dried apricots for raisins. Reduced fat peanut butter and egg substitute lower the fat percentage.

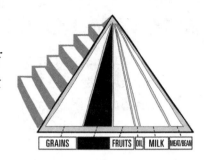

3 tbs. peanut butter
¼ cup chopped raisins
2 tbs. jam
1 tsp. cinnamon
4 slices whole wheat bread
1 egg

¼ cup nonfat (skim) milk
1 tbs. butter substitute (try 'Smart Balance' brand)

Combine peanut butter, raisins, jam and cinnamon. Spread mixture on 2 slices of the bread. Top with remaining bread slices to form a sandwich. In a pie plate or shallow bowl, beat eggs and stir in milk. Dip each sandwich in egg mixture. Melt butter substitute in a skillet. Brown sandwiches on both sides. Makes 2 servings.

per serving   479 calories, 16.9 g protein, 61.3 g carbo., 21.5 g fat, 38% calories from fat

SQUARE MEAL SQUARES

Here's another complete-meal-on-toast.

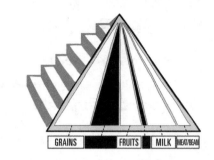

1 cup low-fat cottage cheese
1 tbs. honey, if desired
$^1/_2$ cup chopped walnuts
2 slices whole wheat toast or waffle squares
1 banana, sliced
2 tsp. wheat germ

Combine cottage cheese, honey, if using, and nuts. Spread on toast. Top with banana slices and sprinkle with wheat germ. Makes 2 servings.

per serving   223 calories, 20.2 g protein, 41.6 g carbo., 12.1 g fat, 31% calories from fat

SWEET BREAD

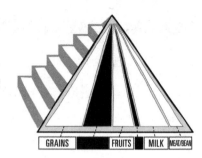

This will make a "breakfast eater" out of everyone. Prepare the cheese mixture the night before. Substitute English muffins for variety.

1 cup low-fat cottage cheese
1/4 cup chopped dates or prunes
1/4 cup chopped walnuts
1 tsp. honey, if desired
1/2 tsp. cinnamon
2 slices whole wheat bread

Mix cheese, dates, nuts, honey, if using, and cinnamon together. Store in the refrigerator. When ready to serve, spread mixture on bread slices. Broil until bubbly. Makes 2 servings.

per serving   356 calories, 21.8 g protein, 43.1 g carbo., 12.6 g fat, 30% calories from fat

CHEESY BREAKFAST SANDWICH

This one's yummy served warm or cold.

2 slices whole wheat bread
$\frac{1}{4}$ cup chutney
2 slices turkey bacon, cooked
2 tbs. grated Parmesan cheese

Spread 1 slice of the bread with chutney. Top with bacon and cheese. Broil until cheese is melted. Cover with second bread slice. Makes 1 sandwich.

per serving   278 calories, 13.4 g protein, 31.5 g carbo., 8.8 g fat, 28% calories from fat

FRUIT-N-CHEESE TOAST

Here's a wholesome American version of a Danish.

1 tbs. butter substitute
2 eggs
1 tbs. 1% low-fat milk
2 tbs. yogurt cheese or nonfat cream cheese
2 slices whole wheat bread
1 small apple, chopped

¼ tsp. lemon juice
2 tbs. raisins

GRAINS FRUITS OIL MILK MEAT/BEAN

Melt butter substitute in an 8-inch square baking pan in a 450° oven. Spread butter substitute evenly in pan. Separate 1 egg. Beat 1 whole egg and 1 egg white with milk. Dip bread in egg mixture, coating both sides. Place in pan. Bake for 5 minutes at 450°. Beat yogurt cheese and remaining egg yolk together. Mix apple, lemon juice and raisins. Remove bread from oven. Spread each slice with cheese mixture and top with fruit mixture. Bake for 5 minutes. Serve warm. Makes 2 servings.

per serving   257 calories, 11.4 g protein, 30 g carbo., 11 g fat, 37% calories from fat

COCONUT TOASTIES

Serve this as a special birthday breakfast surprise. Reduce the amount of coconut or use egg substitute if you're concerned about the fat percentage.

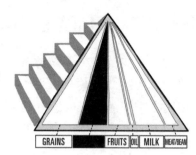

2 eggs
½ cup 1% low-fat milk
½ cup crushed cornflakes
½ cup shredded unsweetened coconut
2 tbs. canola oil

8 slices whole wheat bread
1 can (8 oz.) crushed pineapple, warmed

Beat eggs with milk in a pie plate or shallow bowl. Combine cornflakes and coconut in another pie plate or shallow bowl. Heat oil on a griddle over medium heat. Dip each slice of bread into egg mixture and then into coconut mixture, coating both sides. Cook on griddle until browned on both sides. Serve with warmed pineapple. Makes 4 servings.

per serving   383 calories, 12.7 g protein, 48.9 g carbo., 17.2 g fat, 39% calories from fat

MAKE-BELIEVE WAFFLES

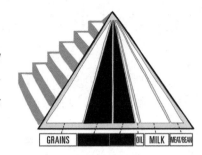

Whole wheat bread makes good "waffles" when you don't have time to make your own. Pick a fresh fruit topping from **Tasty Toppings***, page 112, to add more nutrients and reduce the amount of calories from fat.*

1 egg
¼ cup 1% low-fat milk
1 tbs. butter substitute (try 'Smart Balance' brand), melted
2 slices whole wheat bread

Heat a waffle iron. Combine egg, milk and butter substitute in a pie plate or shallow bowl. Dip bread slices into mixture, one at a time, until well coated. Place bread in waffle iron and close cover. Cook until waffle iron stops steaming and opens easily. Makes 2 servings.

per serving   176 calories, 7.9 g protein, 18.5 g carbo., 8.5 g fat, 42% calories from fat

BANANA FRANCAIS

Fortify your French toast with potassium-rich banana slices and whole grain bread.

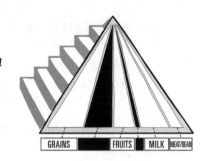

2 eggs
1 banana, chopped
¼ cup 1% low-fat milk
½ tsp. cinnamon
2 tsp. canola oil
4 slices whole wheat bread

Combine eggs, banana, milk and cinnamon in a blender container. Blend until smooth. Pour into a pie plate. Soak bread in banana mixture. Heat oil in a large skillet until hot. Place bread in skillet. Spoon remaining banana mixture over each slice of bread. Cook over medium-high heat until brown on both sides. Makes 2 servings.

per serving   352 calories, 15.2 g protein, 48.8 g carbo., 12.5 g fat, 31% calories from fat

INSTANT BRUNCH

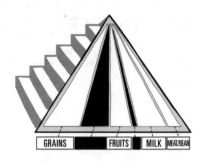

This sandwich is so fun to look at and delicious to eat, kids won't know it's good for them. Use frozen waffles or make your own. If you make your own waffles, use part whole wheat flour and add up to ½ cup of wheat germ. Freeze the extras.

2 tbs. yogurt cheese or nonfat cream cheese
2 tbs. strawberry jam
2 tbs. finely chopped walnuts
2 waffles, toasted

Mix cheese, jam and walnuts. Spread mixture on one of the waffles. Cover with second waffle. Cut into quarters and serve. Makes 2 servings.

per serving   207 calories, 5.3 g protein, 32.3 g carbo., 6.9 g fat, 29% calories from fat

POTPOURRI WAFFLES

*This recipe also makes good pancakes, but it is not necessary to beat the egg whites separately. You can substitute different vegetables if desired. Serve with **Tasty Toppings,** page 112.*

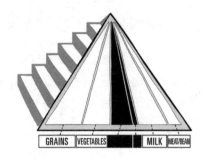

GRAINS | VEGETABLES | MILK | MEAT/BEAN

2 eggs, separated
1 tbs. canola oil
1½ tsp. salt
1 tbs. honey, if desired

1 cup 1% low-fat milk
1 cup whole wheat flour
½ cup shredded carrots
1 cup finely chopped celery

Heat a waffle iron. Mix egg yolks with oil, salt, honey, if using, and milk. Add flour and beat well to blend. Stir in vegetables. Beat egg whites until stiff and fold into batter. Ladle onto waffle iron and close cover. Cook until waffle iron stops steaming and opens easily. Makes 6 to 8 waffles.

per waffle   151 calories, 6.4 g protein, 21.2 g carbo., 5.1 g fat, 29% calories from fat

FUNNY FACE PANCAKES

Cook the pancakes on a nonstick griddle or skillet, or use nonstick cooking spray to prepare the griddle. If desired, use ³/₄ cup egg substitute instead of eggs. Pick a **Tasty Topping,** *page 112.*

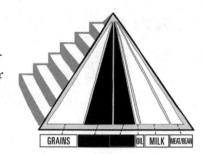

3 eggs
1 cup low-fat cottage cheese
¹/₄ cup flour
dash salt, if desired

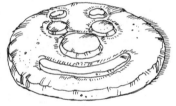

Beat eggs well. Add cottage cheese and beat. Add flour and salt, if using, and mix well. Fill a poultry baster with batter. Make a face with batter on a hot griddle: first the eyes, then nose and mouth. Cook for a few seconds. Ladle more batter over facial features and cook. Turn when brown on the first side. Continue to cook until done. Makes 4 to 6 pancakes.

---

per pancake   90 calories, 8.9 g protein, 5.7 g carbo., 3.3 g fat, 34% calories from fat

PICKY-EATER ZUCCHINI PANCAKES

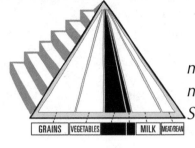

GRAINS | VEGETABLES | MILK | MEAT/BEAN

*Pour the batter on a hot pan or griddle in a free form manner. After serving, ask your child to guess what you made. Whatever he or she guesses, of course, is right! Serve with **Tasty Toppings,** page 112.*

1 small zucchini, sliced
1 1/2 cups flour
3 tsp. baking powder
1/2 tsp. salt, if desired

1 egg, beaten
1 cup 1% low-fat milk
2 tbs. canola oil

Steam zucchini and puree in a blender. Mix with remaining ingredients. Stir just until mixed. Cook pancakes on a hot pan, turning only once. Makes 8 to 10 pancakes.

per pancake   115 calories, 3.6 g protein, 16.3 g carbo., 3.9 g fat, 31% calories from fat

TASTY TOPPINGS

Get out of the butter-and-maple-syrup rut with one of these healthy toppings.

- hot applesauce
- frozen berries, thawed and pureed with juice
- yogurt cheese or nonfat cream cheese, mixed with honey to taste
- flavored yogurt
- jam or preserves
- warm honey
- melted peanut butter (thin with apple juice, if desired)
- fresh fruit puree
- low-fat cottage cheese
- shredded part-skim mozzarella cheese
- low-fat or nonfat cream cheese and fresh fruit
- spiced pineapple: $1/4$ cup crushed pineapple blended with 1 tsp. vanilla extract and $1/4$ tsp. cinnamon

FRUIT-N-CEREAL SQUARES

These make a good breakfast on the run. They have a lot of calories to keep kids going throughout the morning.

3 cups whole wheat flour
2 tsp. baking powder
¼ tsp. salt
3 cups quick oats
¼ cup honey
1½ cups butter substitute (try 'Smart Balance' brand)
2 cups jam or fruit puree

Combine flour, baking powder, salt, oats and honey. Cut in butter substitute until crumbly. Spread ⅔ of mixture on the bottom of an ungreased jelly roll pan (10-x-18-inches). Carefully spread mixture with jam. Sprinkle remaining ingredients over top. Bake at 350° for 30 minutes until lightly browned. Makes 12 servings.

per serving   499 calories, 7.9 g protein, 78.7 g carbo., 19.1 g fat, 33% calories from fat

BREAKFAST BARS

You can substitute rolled oats for the cereal in this high-protein, high-fiber morning square.

1½ cups all-bran or granola cereal
¾ cup flour
1 tsp. baking powder
¼ tsp. salt, optional
¼ cup honey, or to taste
1 banana, mashed

½ cup butter substitute, melted
1 egg
1 tsp. vanilla extract

Set aside ½ cup of the cereal. Combine remaining ingredients in a bowl. Spread mixture into a greased 11-x-7-inch baking dish. Crush reserved cereal and sprinkle over batter. Bake at 350° for 25 minutes. Cool for a few minutes and cut into squares. Makes 12 servings.

per serving   177 calories, 4.1 g protein, 27.4 g carbo., 8.5 g fat, 38% calories from fat

EASY CINNAMON ROLLS

These are sugarless cinnamon rolls. Nonfat cream cheese mixed with apple butter makes a good frosting.

1 loaf (11oz.) frozen bread dough, thawed
1/4 cup butter substitute (try 'Smart Balance' brand)
2 tbs. cinnamon
1 apple, chopped
1 cup raisins
1/2 cups pecans, optional

Roll dough into a 9-x-12-inch rectangle. Spread with butter substitute and sprinkle with cinnamon. Spread chopped apple, raisins and pecans, if desired, over dough. Roll up jelly roll-style. Cut into 1-inch slices. Place slices on a greased cookie sheet and let rise until they have nearly doubled in size. Bake at 350° for 25 to 35 minutes or until brown. Makes 12 servings.

per roll   146 calories, 3 g protein, 24.4 g carbo., 4.8 g fat, 30% calories from fat

BREAKFAST BANANA SPLIT

Make sure kids start the day right by disguising their morning cereal as a dessert. Use fresh fruit that's in season, and always top it off with a cherry.

½ cup low-fat cottage cheese
1 tbs. honey
¼ cup strawberries or raspberries
½ cup low-fat granola

1 banana, halved lengthwise
¼ cup mixed chopped fresh fruit

Mix cottage cheese and honey. Puree berries with a food processor or blender to resemble sauce. Reserve 1 tbs. of the granola. Put remaining granola in 2 banana-split dishes or bowls. Place 1 banana slice over each dish of granola. Scoop cottage cheese mixture with an ice cream scoop into the center of each banana slice. Drizzle berry "sauce" over cottage cheese and bananas. Scatter fresh fruit in dishes. Sprinkle top of cottage cheese with reserved granola to resemble nuts. Makes 2 servings.

per serving   294 calories, 23.2 g protein, 91 g carbo., 18 g fat, 27% calories from fat

MARVELOUS MEALS

118 Serve a "Power" Lunch
119 Cheesy Monkey Sandwich
120 Kewl Kabobs
121 Tuna Triangles
122 Super Spuds
123 Mama Mia Cubes
124 Tomato Balloons
125 Add Pizzazz to Peanut Butter
126 Nutcracker
127 Pinwheels
128 Apple Pie Sandwich
129 Thanksgiving Sandwich
130 Piranha Pita Pocket
131 Fancy Ham Sandwich
132 Ham and Cheese Pillows
133 Veggie Pillows
134 Mozzarella Muffins
135 New England Muffins
136 Nacho Sandwich
137 Tuna Boats
138 Pizza Gobbler
139 Bahama Bagels
140 Add Temptation to Tuna
141 Tuna Pillows
142 Popovers
143 Tunaroni Stuffers
144 Kingfish Stuffers
145 Scrapple Stuffers
146 Chinese Chicken Stuffers
147 Turkey Circles
148 Popeye Burgers
149 Corny Pudding
150 Popeye's Pie
151 Mexican Wieners
152 Skinny Dips
153 Eat Your Spinach
154 Spaghetti Salad
155 Petite Apple Tarts

SERVE A "POWER" LUNCH

Whether you have a preschooler who still has lunch at home or an older child who takes lunch to school, adding variety, excitement and a little color to lunch foods will get results you won't believe. Even if your little one doesn't go to school, occasionally pack lunch in a lunch box and see how it increases his or her interest in eating.

If you plan ahead, it takes only minutes to prepare something delicious and nutritious. Every meal can be something your child looks forward to. Try different combinations from various recipes in this chapter for more variety. Select a snack from Super Snacks to add to the lunch box fixings and complete the meal with one of the Dynamite Drinks for the vacuum bottle.

Help your child become more interested in trying new dishes by serving them with flair. No one has to know that tucked into an old favorite is a food usually left untouched. If spaghetti is a favorite, sneak a little tuna or zucchini into the sauce. Introduce it by talking about Italy and the children who live there. This gives the new dish a special image and your child not only learns about new foods, but also about new places and people. Who could resist trying something with all that going for it?

CHEESY MONKEY SANDWICH

An odd—and delicious—combination

GRAINS FRUITS MILK

1 banana
1 tsp. lemon juice
3 tbs. cottage cheese
2 slices raisin bread

Mash banana and lemon juice with fork. Stir in cottage cheese and spread on raisin bread to make sandwich. Serves 1.

per serving   192 calories, 8.5 g protein, 38.0 g carbo., 1.8 g fat, 16 calories from fat

KEWL KABOBS

Lunch doesn't have to be a sandwich.

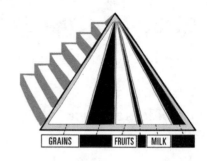

1 apple, peach, banana, or pear, cut into cubes
6 pretzel sticks
Swiss, jack, or cheddar cheese, cut into cubes

Push a piece of fruit on one end of the pretzel and a piece of cheese on the other end.

Optional: add a cube of ham. Serves 6

per serving   88 calories, 4.8 g protein, 3.4 g carbo., 6.3 g fat, 57 calories from fat

TUNA TRIANGLES

A different way to use tuna.

1 pkg. (10 oz.) corn bread mix
1 can (6 oz.) tuna, packed in water, drained

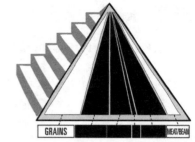

Prepare corn bread batter according to package direc-
tions. Add tuna and mix well. Pour into greased 15-by-10-by-1-inch jelly-roll pan.
Bake at 400° for 15 to 20 minutes. Cut into 36 triangles. Makes 3 dozen small bites.
Serves 6

per serving   241 calories, 11.8 g protein, 28.9 g carbo., 8.3 g fat, 75 calories from fat

SUPER SPUDS

Fill a tater with anything your child likes!

1 small potato (or sweet potato)
1/2 cup broccoli (or other vegetable)
1/4 cup shredded cheddar cheese (or other cheese)
2 strips of cooked bacon or cut up ham

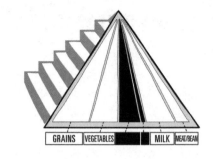

Bake potato until tender. Slit open potato, let your child add toppings, and enjoy.

per serving   566 calories, 32.7 g protein, 33.8 g carbo., 6.3 g fat, 300 calories from fat

MAMA MIA CUBES

These are best when served cold. Secure cubes with frilly toothpicks. Remove picks if serving them to small children, or replace them with pretzel sticks just before serving.

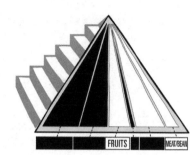

8 thin slices extra-lean ham
1 medium cantaloupe

Cut ham into 1-inch strips. Cut cantaloupe into cubes. Wrap a ham strip around each cantaloupe cube and secure with toothpicks. Chill and serve. Makes 4 servings.

per serving   121 calories, 12.2 g protein, 11.7 g carbo., 3.2 g fat, 23% calories from fat

TOMATO BALLOONS

These make a nice alternative to sandwiches. Kids will feel like grown-ups while they are eating them.

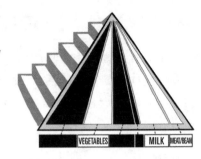

1 medium tomato
¼ cup low-fat cottage cheese
¼ cup water-packed tuna, drained

Cut stem end off tomato and scoop out insides. Mix cottage cheese and tuna. Stuff into tomato. Makes 1 serving.

per serving   132 calories, 21.4 g protein, 7.7 g carbo., 1.7 g fat, 12% calories from fat

ADD PIZZAZZ TO PEANUT BUTTER

Although peanut butter is delicious and nutritious, it gets about 70% of its calories from fat. Try a reduced fat version which brings fat content down to about 55%. If your child's plain peanut butter sandwich needs some liveliness, try adding one or more of the following.

- chopped apple
- applesauce
- grated carrots
- chopped celery
- grated low-fat or nonfat cheese
- minced cooked chicken breast
- unsweetened shredded coconut
- low-fat cottage cheese
- yogurt cheese or nonfat cream cheese
- chopped dates
- extra-lean ham
- chopped dried fruit
- sliced pears
- crushed pineapple
- raisins
- crushed raspberries
- sesame seeds
- sprouts
- sunflower kernels
- diced tomatoes

NUTCRACKER

This mixture can also be served with carrot sticks and pear slices for dipping.

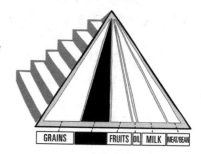

1/2 cup yogurt cheese or nonfat cream cheese
1/4 cup crushed pineapple, well drained
1/4 cup chopped pecans
whole wheat crackers

Mix cheese, pineapple and pecans. Spread on wheat crackers. Makes 1 cup.

per 1/4 cup filling   55.5 calories, 2.8 g protein, 6.3 g carbo., 2.4 g fat, 37% calories from fat

PINWHEELS

Make these ahead of time and use as needed.

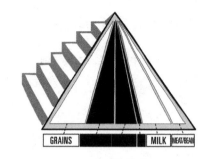

$1/2$ cup yogurt cheese or nonfat cream cheese, softened
1 tsp. Worcestershire sauce
$1/2$ tsp. chopped chives
$1/4$ tsp. dry mustard
6 thin slices extra-lean ham
3 slices rye bread

Blend cheese, Worcestershire sauce, chives and mustard. Spread over ham slices and roll up jelly roll-style. Chill and cut into slices. Serve with rye bread. Makes 2 to 3 servings.

per serving   146 calories, 14.4 g protein, 15 g carbo., 3.1 g fat, 19% calories from fat

APPLE PIE SANDWICH

It contains fruit and vegetables, it's high in protein--yet is still tastes like dessert.

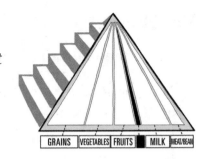

GRAINS VEGETABLES FRUITS MILK MEAT/BEAN

¹/₄ cup yogurt cheese or nonfat cream cheese
2 tbs. chopped walnuts
2 tbs. chopped celery
3 tbs. chopped apple
1 tsp. cinnamon
4 slices raisin bread

Mix cheese, walnuts, celery, apple and cinnamon. Spread on 2 slices of the raisin bread. Top with remaining bread slices. Makes 2 servings.

per serving   197 calories, 7.2 g protein, 34.5 g carbo., 3.9 g fat, 17% calories from fat

THANKSGIVING SANDWICH

This sandwich lets you celebrate turkey day any time.

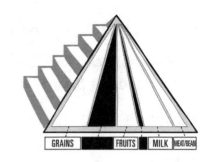

½ cup chopped cooked turkey
2–3 tbs. yogurt cheese or nonfat cream cheese
2 tbs. cranberry sauce
4 slices whole wheat bread

Mix turkey with cheese and cranberry sauce. Spread on 2 slices of the bread. Top with remaining bread slices. Makes 2 servings.

per serving   334 calories, 19.3 g protein, 40.7 g carbo., 11.7 g fat, 30% calories from fat

PIRANHA PITA POCKET

Sardines are a good source of calcium. Substitute water-packed tuna, if desired.

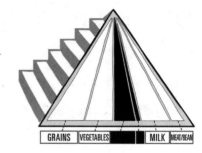

4 sardines, chopped
2 tbs. sweet pickle relish
2 tbs. reduced fat mayonnaise
1/4 cup grated Monterey Jack cheese
2 small pita breads

Mix sardines, relish, mayonnaise and cheese. Cut a 1-inch section from one side of each pita bread to open a pocket. Place cut section of bread inside pocket. Spoon sardine mixture into pita pockets. Makes 2 servings.

per serving   309 calories, 15.8 g protein, 39 g carbo., 9.9 g fat, 29% calories from fat

FANCY HAM SANDWICH

The combination of bright colors and fancy designs in this sandwich will entice the kids to eat it all.

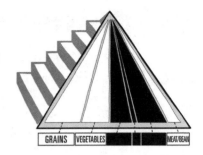

2 drops food coloring
1 tbs. 1% low-fat milk
4 slices oatmeal bread
¼ cup cooked peas, mashed
3 oz. extra-lean ham, finely chopped
2 tbs. reduced fat mayonnaise

Mix food coloring with milk and lightly paint a design on 2 slices of the bread. Toast all bread slices lightly. Mix peas with ham and mayonnaise. Spread mixture on the plain toast slices and top with decorated slices, design-side up. Makes 2 servings.

per serving   267 calories, 17.1 g protein, 38 g carbo., 6.3 g fat, 20% calories from fat

HAM AND CHEESE PILLOWS

Substitute chopped cooked chicken breast for ham and add a little celery for crunch.

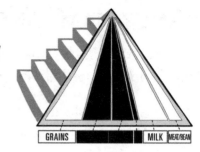

3 oz. extra-lean ham, finely chopped
1 tbs. reduced fat mayonnaise
1/4 cup grated Monterey Jack cheese
2 small pita breads

Mix ham, mayonnaise and cheese. Cut a 1-inch section from one side of each pita bread to open a pocket. Place cut sections of bread inside pockets. Spoon ham mixture into pita pockets. Makes 2 servings.

per serving   294 calories, 18.1 g protein, 34.2 g carbo., 9.2 g fat, 28% calories from fat

VEGGIE PILLOWS

Use a combination of chopped celery, carrots, green peppers and mushrooms for a crunchy, colorful lunch.

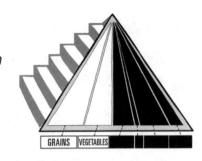

GRAINS | VEGETABLES

¹/₄ cup bean sprouts
¹/₄ cup chopped vegetables
1 tbs. ranch-style salad dressing
1 small pita bread

Combine bean sprouts, chopped vegetables and dressing in a bowl. Cut a 1-inch section from one side of pita bread to open a pocket. Place cut sections of bread inside pockets. Stuff veggie mixture into pita pocket. Makes 1 to 2 servings.

per serving   227 calories, 7.2 g protein, 35.2 g carbo., 6.6 g fat, 26% calories from fat

MOZZARELLA MUFFINS

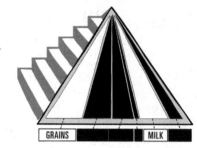

French or rye bread rounds make good substitutes for English muffins.

¼ cup grated part-skim mozzarella cheese
2 tbs. reduced fat mayonnaise
2 English muffins, halved

Mix cheese with mayonnaise and spread on muffin halves. Broil until cheese is bubbly. Makes 2 servings.

per serving   196 calories, 8.1 g protein, 27.3 g carbo., 5.3 g fat, 25% calories from fat

NEW ENGLAND MUFFINS

Stick two of these together and tuck them into the lunch box.

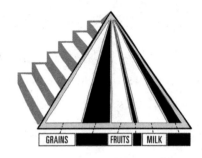

¼ cup grated cheddar cheese
¼ cup grated apple
2 English muffins, halved

Mix together cheese and apples. Sprinkle evenly on muffin halves. Broil until bubbly or bake at 350° for 10 minutes. Makes 2 servings.

per serving   205 calories, 8.1 g protein, 28.5 g carbo., 5.8 g fat, 26% calories from fat

NACHO SANDWICH

Instead of sour cream, garnish this with yogurt cheese diluted with a little nonfat (skim) milk. Look for low-fat or nonfat refried beans. They're often labeled vegetarian.

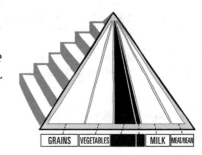

2 flour tortillas, warmed
1/2 cup vegetarian refried beans, heated
1/4 cup grated cheddar cheese
1/4 cup shredded lettuce
1/4 cup chopped tomato

Spread tortillas evenly with beans. Top equally with remaining ingredients. Fold over one end of each tortilla and roll up sideways. Makes 2 servings.

per serving   224 calories, 10.2 g protein, 31 g carbo., 7.7 g fat, 30% calories from fat

TUNA BOATS

Add seeds, grated carrots, chopped celery or pickle relish to tuna mixture for an added attraction. Cheddar cheese triangles make neat sails. Or use fat carrots thinly sliced lengthwise and cut into triangles.

1 can (6½ oz.) water-packed tuna, drained
1½ tbs. plain low-fat yogurt
1 small green bell pepper

Mix tuna with yogurt and any other desired ingredients. Cut green pepper in half (or in quarters for a small child), lengthwise. Remove seeds and membranes. Fill with tuna mixture. Add sails, if desired. Makes 2 servings.

per serving   137 calories, 25.8 g protein, 6.3 g carbo., 0.6 g fat, 4% calories from fat

PIZZA GOBBLER

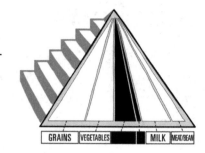

Use your child's favorite vegetable as an additional topping.

¹/₂ cup pizza sauce
4 English muffins, halved
¹/₄ cup grated part-skim mozzarella cheese
1 turkey frankfurter, sliced

Spread sauce evenly on muffin halves. Sprinkle each half with cheese and top with frankfurter slices. Broil until cheese is bubbly. Makes 4 servings.

per serving   217 calories, 8.4 g protein, 31.5 g carbo., 5.7 g fat, 24% calories from fat

BAHAMA BAGELS

Offer your brown-bagger this nice change of pace.

GRAINS FRUITS MILK MEAT/BEAN

¹/₂ cup low-fat cottage cheese
1 tsp. chopped walnuts
1 tsp. crushed pineapple
2 bagels, halved

Mix cheese, pineapple and nuts. Spread between bagel slices. Makes 2 servings.

per serving   245 calories, 15.1 g protein, 37.7 g carbo., 3.3 g fat, 12% calories from fat

ADD TEMPTATION TO TUNA

Tired tuna can be made tasty and tempting with a few of these additions.

- sliced almonds
- chopped apples
- cooked and crumbled turkey bacon
- green beans
- bean sprouts
- chopped celery
- shredded cabbage
- grated low-fat or nonfat cheese
- chow mein noodles
- cooked pasta

- grapes
- diced bell peppers
- Mandarin orange segments
- peas
- pickle slices
- crushed pineapple
- diced tomatoes
- yogurt cheese or nonfat cream cheese
- chopped walnuts
- sliced water chestnuts

TUNA PILLOWS

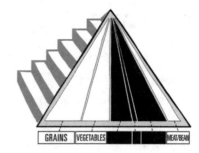

Cornbread, onions and olives enliven traditional tuna casserole.

1 pkg. (10 oz.) cornbread mix
1 tbs. dehydrated minced onion
1 can (6½ oz.) water-packed tuna, drained
¼ cup chopped black olives

Prepare cornbread batter according to package directions. Stir in tuna and onion. Pour into a greased 10-x-15-inch jelly roll pan. Scatter olives over top. Bake at 400° for 15 to 20 minutes. Cut into squares. Makes 12 servings.

per serving   103 calories, 6.3 g protein, 12.4 g carbo., 3.1 g fat, 27% calories from fat

POPOVERS

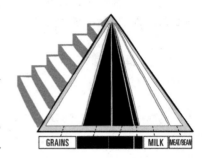

Here's a way to present a lunch that fascinates children. Popovers lend themselves to any kind of spread and they tempt a child to try something different. Liquid egg substitute reduces fat and cholesterol and keeps well in the refrigerator or freezer. Serve popovers hot with your favorite spread. Split them open to stuff with filling.

1 cup flour
$\frac{1}{2}$ tsp. salt

1 cup 1% low-fat milk
$\frac{1}{2}$ cup egg substitute, or 2 eggs

Spray muffin cups well with nonstick cooking spray. Place in a 425° oven to heat. Beat ingredients together just until smooth. Fill heated muffin cups $\frac{3}{4}$ full. Bake for 40 to 45 minutes or until golden brown. Do not open oven during baking. Serve immediately or fill with a savory filling. Makes 6 popovers.

per popover   102 calories, 5.1 g protein, 17 g carbo., 1 g fat, 11% calories from fat

TUNARONI STUFFERS

This high protein, high carbohydrate meal provides lots of energy for active kids. Make them laugh by using funny pasta shapes instead of macaroni.

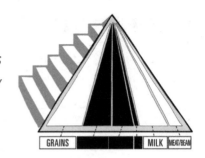

1 can (6½ oz.) water-packed tuna, drained
1 cup cooked macaroni
2½ tbs. plain low-fat yogurt
½ tbs. mustard
4 *Popovers*, page 142

Combine tuna, macaroni, yogurt and mustard. Spoon into popovers. Serve immediately. Makes 4 servings.

---

per serving   206 calories, 18.2 g protein, 22.7 g carbo., 4.1 g fat, 18% calories from fat

---

KINGFISH STUFFERS

Any filling tastes twice as good served in a popover shell.

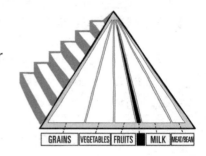

1 can (6½ oz.) water-packed tuna, drained
2 tbs. plain low-fat yogurt
1 tbs. chopped apple
1 tbs. grated carrots
1 tbs. raisins
4 *Popovers*, page 142

Combine tuna, yogurt, apple, carrot and raisins. Fill popovers with mixture. Serve immediately. Makes 4 servings.

per serving 162 calories, 16.4 g protein, 14.8 g carbo., 3.8 g fat, 22% calories from fat

SCRAPPLE STUFFERS

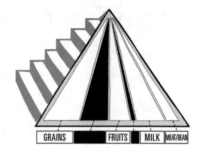

Apple butter contains no butter at all. It is made by slowly cooking together apples, spices and cider.

1/4 cup apple butter
1/4 cup grated cheddar cheese
4 *Popovers*, page 142

Heat apple butter gently in a small saucepan. Divide apple butter equally among warm popovers. Top with cheese. Serve immediately. Makes 4 servings.

per serving   77 calories, 2.4 g protein, 10.3 g carbo., 3.1 g fat, 35% calories from fat

CHINESE CHICKEN STUFFERS

Feeding your kids exotic flavors when they are young will make them adventurous eaters as adults.

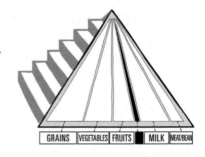

GRAINS   VEGETABLES   FRUITS   MILK   MEAT/BEAN

¹/₂ cup chopped cooked chicken
2-3 tbs. drained crushed pineapple
¹/₄ cup chopped snow peas
2 tbs. plain nonfat yogurt
¹/₄ cup chow mein noodles
4 *Popovers*, page 142

Combine chicken, pineapple, snow peas and yogurt in a small saucepan. Heat on low until just warmed through. Remove from heat and stir in noodles. Fill warm popovers and serve immediately. Makes 4 servings.

per serving   159 calories, 9.7 g protein, 16.7 g carbo., 5.8 g fat, 33% calories from fat

TURKEY CIRCLES

Hot dogs in hamburger buns? This special cooking technique will leave your kids wondering, "How did she do that?"

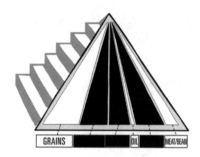

4 turkey frankfurters
4 hamburger buns
1 can (8 oz.) baked beans

Slash each frankfurter crosswise at ½-inch intervals, cutting halfway through. Broil or barbecue frankfurter until it curls into a circle and is heated through. Toast buns. Place a frankfurter circle on the bottom half of each bun. Fill centers of circles with 2 tbs. baked beans. Cover with top bun. Serve remaining beans as a side dish. Makes 4 servings.

per serving   285 calories, 13.1 g protein, 34.2 g carbo., 10.9 g fat, 34% calories from fat

POPEYE BURGERS

Use any vegetable to enrich burgers. It's sneaky, but it works!

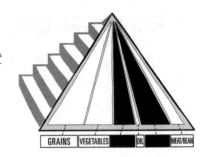

1 cup spinach
1 lb. ground turkey
6 hamburger buns

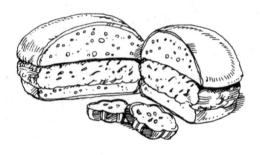

Steam spinach and puree with a blender. Add to ground turkey and mix lightly but well. Form into patties and broil. Serve on toasted buns. Makes 6 servings.

per serving   304 calories, 22.4 g protein, 22.8 g carbo., 12.8 g fat, 39% calories from fat

CORNY PUDDING

Here's an unusual way to serve a popular vegetable. Most major brands offer canned vegetables without added salt. If you buy regular canned vegetables, rinse them first to remove excess salt.

2 eggs
1 cup water
1 can (16 oz.) whole kernel corn
1 cup dates, finely chopped

Lightly beat eggs in a bowl. Add water and stir to blend. Place corn and dates in a saucepan. Stir in egg mixture. Cook over low heat for 15 minutes. Pour into a blender container. Blend on high speed until smooth. Return to saucepan and cook for 10 minutes, stirring constantly. Pour into individual serving dishes and chill in refrigerator. Makes 4 servings.

per serving   251 calories, 7 g protein, 53.8 g carbo., 3.8 g fat, 12% calories from fat

POPEYE'S PIE

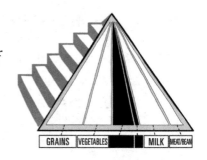

This was the one that made a spinach lover out of Popeye.

1 pkg. (10 oz.) refrigerator pizza dough
1 lb. fresh spinach, steamed, or frozen spinach, thawed
1 egg
1/3 cup wheat germ
1/4 cup grated Swiss or cheddar cheese
1 tsp. Worcestershire sauce
pinch garlic powder

Heat oven to 400°. Unroll pizza dough. Reshape dough to line a 9-inch pie pan. Combine spinach, egg, wheat germ, cheese, Worcestershire sauce and garlic powder. Pour into pizza shell. Bake for 25 minutes. Cut into wedges. Makes 6 servings.

per serving   188 calories, 9.7 g protein, 27.7 g carbo., 4.9 g fat, 23% calories from fat

MEXICAN WIENERS

This one is fun for the kids to make and eat. Serve with mild salsa.

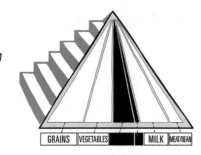

1 turkey frankfurter
2 tbs. vegetarian refried beans
1/4 cup shredded lettuce
1 tbs. grated cheddar cheese
1 flour or corn tortilla

Cook turkey frankfurter according to package directions. Spread refried beans on tortilla. Sprinkle with lettuce and cheese. Place frankfurter close to one side. Roll tortilla around frankfurter. Warm in a microwave or oven and serve. Or serve at room temperature. Makes 1 serving.

per serving   266 calories, 12.7 g protein, 25.9 g carbo., 13.1 g fat, 43% calories from fat

SKINNY DIPS

My son could eat these every night! Now he helps me pre-pare them.

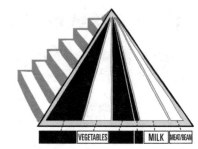

4 large potatoes, baked
1/2 cup grated part-skim mozzarella cheese
2 oz. extra-lean ham, diced
1 green onion, chopped   1/2 cup ranch-style salad dressing

Cut potatoes in half lengthwise. Scoop out most of potato and reserve for another recipe. Sprinkle cheese, ham and green onion over skins. Heat in a 350° oven for 4 to 5 minutes, until cheese is bubbly. Serve with dressing as dip. Makes 4 servings.

per serving   396 calories, 12.6 g protein, 55.6 g carbo., 14.5 g fat, 32% calories from fat

For *Mexican Skinny Dips*, sprinkle potato skins with mozzarella, 2 slices cooked and crumbled turkey sausage and 1 chopped green onion. Dip in salsa.

For *PIzza Skinny Dips*, sprinkle skins with mozzarella, 1/4 cup grated Parmesan , 2 oz. diced turkey salami and 1 chopped green onion. Dip in pizza sauce.

EAT YOUR SPINACH

Substitute broccoli for spinach or try another vegetable. Prepare the casserole with nonstick cooking spray to keep the fat content low. Add a little 1% low-fat milk to the spinach mixture if it appears to thick.

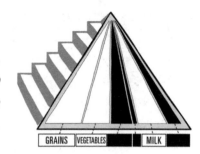

1 pkg. (10 oz.) frozen chopped spinach
1 pkg. (3 oz.) nonfat cream cheese, softened
1/2 cup breadcrumbs
1/4 cup grated Parmesan cheese
1 tsp. salt, or to taste

Cook spinach according to package directions. Drain well. Mix spinach, cream cheese and salt. Place in a greased casserole. Toss breadcrumbs and cheese in a bowl. Sprinkle over spinach mixture. Bake at 350° for 30 minutes. Makes 4 servings.

per serving   121 calories, 8.8 g protein, 16.4 g carbo., 2.7 g fat, 19% calories from fat

SPAGHETTI SALAD

Here's an Italian way of serving vegetables. Top with grated Parmesan cheese if desired. Use whole wheat or vegetable spaghetti for variety. Use any combination of sliced cooked carrots, zucchini, green beans, green pepper or other favorites for the vegetables.

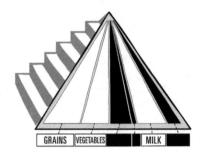

½ cups plain nonfat yogurt
1 tbs. lemon juice
1 tsp. Italian seasoning herbs
½ lb. spaghetti, cooked and drained

½ cup chopped celery
2 tbs. chopped green onion, if desired
2 cups sliced cooked vegetables

Mix yogurt, lemon juice and herbs together well. Combine spaghetti, celery, green onion, if using, and vegetables in a large mixing bowl. Toss with yogurt mixture. Chill before serving. Makes 4 to 6 servings.

per serving   185 calories, 10.4 g protein, 35.5 g carbo., 0.7 g fat, 3% calories from fat

PETITE APPLE TARTS

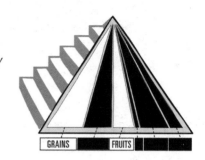

Complaints from the family that there's never any dessert? Try these easy, low-fat treats.

2 tbs. cornstarch
1 tsp. cinnamon
1/4 tsp. nutmeg
1 cup frozen apple juice concentrate
1 tbs. lemon juice
1 tbs. butter substitute (try 'Smart Balance' brand)

6 cups sliced unpeeled apples
6 individual graham cracker crusts

Blend cornstarch, cinnamon, nutmeg, apple juice concentrate and lemon juice together in a saucepan. Cook over medium heat until thickened. Add butter substitute. Divide apple slices evenly in crusts. Pour slightly cooled apple juice mixture over apples. Bake in a 350° oven for 30 to 40 minutes. Makes 6 servings.

per serving   477 calories, 3 g protein, 81.5 g carbo., 17.1 g fat, 31% calories from fat

Serve Creative, Easy, Nutritious Meals with **nitty gritty®** Cookbooks

1 or 2, Cooking for
100 Dynamite Desserts
9 x 13 Pan Cookbook
Asian Cooking
Bagels, Best
Barbecue Cookbook
Beer and Good Food
Big Book Bread Machine
Big Book Kitchen Appliance
Big Book Snack, Appetizer
Blender Drinks
Bread Baking
New Bread Machine Book
Bread Machine III
Bread Machine V
Bread Machine VI
Bread Machine, Entrees
Burger Bible
Cappuccino/Espresso
Casseroles
Chicken, Unbeatable
Chile Peppers

Cooking in Clay
Convection Oven
Cook-Ahead Cookbook
Crockery Pot, Extra-Special
Deep Fryer
Dehydrator Cookbook
Dessert Fondues
Edible Gifts
Edible Pockets
Fabulous Fiber Cookery
Fondue and Hot Dips
Fondue, New International
Freezer, 'Fridge, Pantry
Garlic Cookbook
Grains, Cooking with
Healthy Cooking on Run
Ice Cream Maker
Irish Pub Cooking
Italian, Quick and Easy
Juicer Book II
Kids, Cooking with Your
Kids, Healthy Snacks for

Loaf Pan, Recipes for
Low-Carb
No Salt No Sugar No Fat
Party Foods/Appetizers
Pasta Machine Cookbook
Pasta, Quick and Easy
Pinch of Time
Pizza, Best
Porcelain, Cooking in
Pressure Cooker
Rice Cooker
Salmon Cookbook
Sandwich Maker
Simple Substitutions
Slow Cooking
Soups and Stews
Soy & Tofu Recipes
Tapas Fantásticas
Toaster Oven Cookbook
Waffles & Pizzelles
Wedding Catering book
Wraps and Roll-Ups

"Millions of books sold—for more than 35 years"   **For a free catalog, call: Bristol Publishing Enterprises**
(800) 346-4889 • www.bristolpublishing.com